OPERATION *TYPHOON*

CASEMATE | ILLUSTRATED

CASEMATE | ILLUSTRATED

OPERATION *TYPHOON*

THE GERMAN ASSAULT ON MOSCOW, 1941

PHILIPPE NAUD

⊙ CASEMATE | ILLUSTRATED

MILITARIA

CIS0008

Print Edition: ISBN 978-1-61200-6710
Digital Edition: ISBN 978-1-61200-6727

This book is published in cooperation with and under license from
Sophia Histoire & Collections. Originally published in French as
Militaria Hors-Serie No 105, © Histoire & Collections 2017

Typeset, design and additional material © Casemate Publishers 2018
Translation by Myriam Bell
Design by Paul Hewitt, Battlefield Design
Color artwork by Laurent Lecoq © Histoire & Collections
Original cartography by Morgan Gillard
Photo retouching and separations by Remy Spezzano
Printed and bound by Megaprint, Turkey

CASEMATE PUBLISHERS (US)
Telephone (610) 853-9131
Fax (610) 853-9146
Email: casemate@casematepublishers.com
www.casematepublishers.com

CASEMATE PUBLISHERS (UK)
Telephone (01865) 241249
Fax (01865) 794449
Email: casemate-uk@casematepublishers.co.uk
www.casematepublishers.co.uk

Title page: The German Army in 1941 remained dependent on horsepower.
The soldiers wear the *zeltbahn*, an individual, camouflage tent canvas that
could also be used as a raincoat. (Walter Luben/ECPAD/Defense)
Contents page: The 76.2mm M1927 gun equipped an infantry gun battery
in each Russian regiment, those of the cavalry having to make do with two
pieces. It was another excellent weapon, superior to the infantry support
gun deployed by the Heer and therefore re-used by German infantry. The
man in the center wears the *budenovka*, a headdress going back to the
Civil War and progressively replaced by the *ushanka* winter hat. (Ph. Rio
Collection)

Please note: armored vehicles and vehicles illustrations are not to scale.

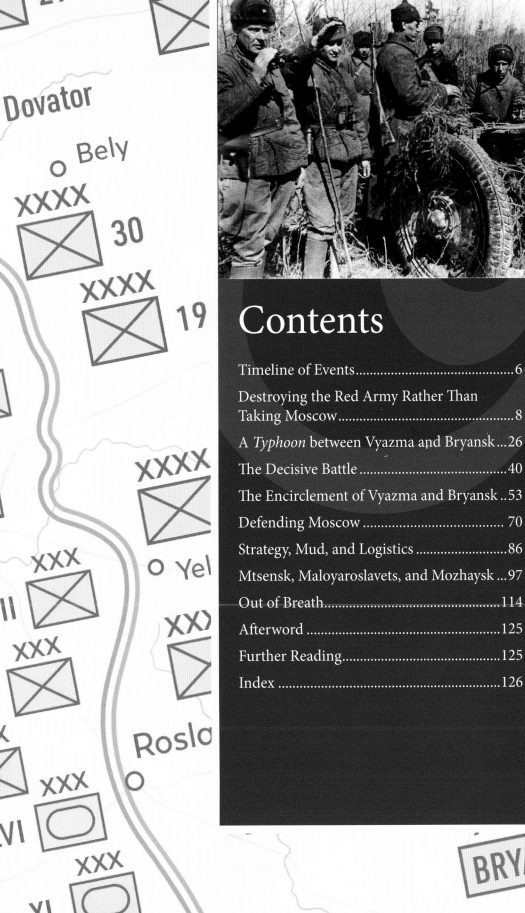

Contents

Timeline of Events

On June 22, 1941, 99 German divisions launched Operation *Barbarossa*, the German invasion of the Soviet Union. Hitler expected a swift victory, with the Red Army destroyed and key objectives seized long before winter arrived. Although the encirclement battles of Minsk, Smolensk and Kiev resulted in 1.2 million Russian soldiers taken prisoner, many casualties, and thousands of tanks and aircraft destroyed or captured, it was not until September that Hitler announced an operation against the army group defending Moscow, capital of the USSR.

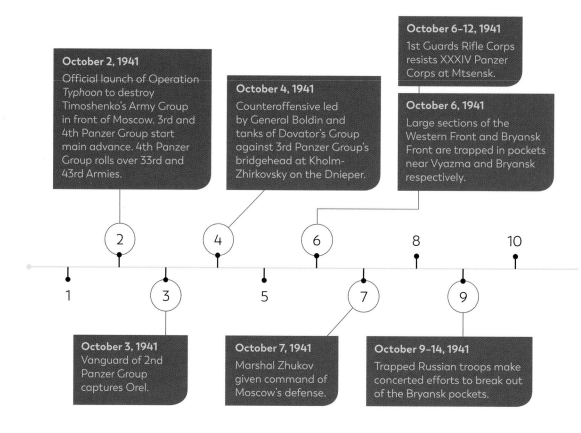

October 2, 1941
Official launch of Operation *Typhoon* to destroy Timoshenko's Army Group in front of Moscow. 3rd and 4th Panzer Group start main advance. 4th Panzer Group rolls over 33rd and 43rd Armies.

October 4, 1941
Counteroffensive led by General Boldin and tanks of Dovator's Group against 3rd Panzer Group's bridgehead at Kholm-Zhirkovsky on the Dnieper.

October 6–12, 1941
1st Guards Rifle Corps resists XXXIV Panzer Corps at Mtsensk.

October 6, 1941
Large sections of the Western Front and Bryansk Front are trapped in pockets near Vyazma and Bryansk respectively.

October 3, 1941
Vanguard of 2nd Panzer Group captures Orel.

October 7, 1941
Marshal Zhukov given command of Moscow's defense.

October 9–14, 1941
Trapped Russian troops make concerted efforts to break out of the Bryansk pockets.

A detachment of BA-10M armored cars takes a break in a forest, to check their map. These powerful vehicles had no equivalent on the German side. According to the organization and equipment tables, tank brigades were allocated three armored cars, often BA-10s. (G. Gorokhoff Collection)

October 12–17, 1941
Battle of Borodino ends in Russian defeat.

October 18, 1941
Mozhaysk abandoned by 5th Army and taken by Kampfgruppe von Bülow.

October 20, 1941
Southern Bryansk pocket reduced.

12 14 16 18 20

11 13 15 17 19

October 11/12, 1941
Some of Western Front manages to escape the Vyazma pocket.

October 14, 1941
Vyazma battle announced as over, Army Group Center claims it has taken over half a million Russian prisoners.

Kalinin taken by XLI Panzer Corps.

Destroying the Red Army Rather Than Taking Moscow

During the first weeks of Operation *Barbarossa*, the capture of Moscow was only a secondary objective. In contrast to the feelings of his staff, Hitler prioritized the destruction of the Red Army and control of the USSR's considerable resources over tackling the emblems of the Soviet regime. Despite the best efforts of his generals and the Wehrmacht Ostheer (the German Army of the Eastern Front), it was not until September 6, 1941 that the Führer was able to announce in Directive no. 36 that the recent victories had created "the conditions to conduct a decisive operation against Timoshenko's army group, who is leading unsuccessful defensive operations on Army Group Center's front. It must be destroyed once and for all before winter."

T-26 wrecks lying in a field, summer 1941. The one in the foreground seems to be a 1939 model. Nearly 1,900 T-26s were serving in the Western Front sector on June 22, compared to 475 at the beginning of *Typhoon* in late September. (Unknown photographer/ECPAD/Defense)

Trucks, including a GAZ seized from the Red Army, bypass the wrecks of a T-26 and a T-34 M1941. As modern as the T-34 was, it did not perform that well at the beginning of *Barbarossa*, contributing to a certain complacency from the Ostheer towards this menace. (Unknown photographer/ECPAD/Defense)

In early September 1941 the armies of the Third Reich and its allies seemed to have the upper hand even though the initial schedule for *Barbarossa* had not been kept—Moscow had not been taken on August 15, and the war was probably going to carry on beyond November 1. In contrast, the USSR had been suffering ever since June 22. The Red Army had been driven out of the Baltic countries, from most of Ukraine and from a large part of Belarus. The huge encirclement battles of Minsk and Smolensk in July, and Kiev in mid-September delivered 1.2 million prisoners to the Germans. Almost all of the mechanized corps deployed in the west of the USSR—who were supposed to have stopped the panzer divisions, or even taken the war into enemy territory—had been annihilated.

This series of victories explains in part, not only the German staff's optimism, but also Hitler's wish to prioritize the destruction of Timoshenko's army group over the capture of Moscow. In September Marshal Semyon Timoshenko was in the south of the USSR. His "group" was in fact three distinct army groups, known as fronts—the Western, Bryansk, and Reserve Fronts. The three Fronts were positioned within 300km of Moscow, covering the western approaches to the capital.

Consequently, the Oberkommando des Heeres—the High Command of the German Army, OKH—and Army Group Center began to plan one of the largest offensives of the war. However, the massive encirclement at Kiev—which involved part of Army Group Center—the weather, and logistics issues delayed Operation *Typhoon*. In its final form, the plan called for *Typhoon* to be launched at the end of September. Three panzer groups and three armies

This T-26 has taken a direct hit, and is beyond repair. (Unknown photographer/ECPAD/Defense)

would surround the Bryansk and Vyazma Fronts, and open a substantial breach in front of Moscow. However, the details of capturing Moscow were not covered in the plan, another sign of OKH's optimism. Why worry? The Germans had more men—an overall ratio of one to two—and a better equipped and trained army, in every way superior to the despised and depleted Workers' and Peasants' Red Army.

Army Group Center appeared to be at its peak. Despite some problems around Smolensk, including abandoning the salient of Yelnya in early September, the victories had been piling up since June. It had seen greater results than the two other army groups, both of which had faced setbacks and delays. Army Group Center in contrast had moved from one encirclement battle to the next—one at the end of June near Białystok, then Minsk, all the way to Smolensk a month later. Even the "defeat" of Yelnya resulted in over 30,000 Russian casualties compared to fewer than 6,000 for the Ostheer. Nevertheless, the men of Army Group Center were weary. On average, its divisions were still 75 percent strength, but the replacement system was beginning to fail—on average only one replacement was being sent for every two losses. The situation with equipment was better, except for motorized units, as vehicles were suffering not only from attrition, but also due to the wear and tear caused by the bad roads. For example, Guderian's 2nd Panzer Group had fought almost continuously whilst also covering huge distances. It was only able to take a few days' break between the end of the fighting around the Kiev pocket and the beginning of *Typhoon*. Globally, the logistics situation showed some serious flaws.

Field Marshal Fedor von Bock in conversation with his officers at the end of summer 1941. Von Bock supervised the initial plans for *Typhoon* and it is said that for this purpose he even flew over Moscow. (Unknown photographer/ECPAD/Defense)

Was the Ostheer Confident or Deluded?

While a number of officers involved in *Barbarossa* may have spared a thought for Napoleon's ill-fated Russian campaign in 1812, German commanders retained a certain level of optimism, even arrogance, despite delays to the *Barbarossa* agenda. Optimism had obviously been widespread on the eve of *Barbarossa*, though not often as rampant as that of Captain Hauptmann of the 6th Panzer Division, who, basing his calculation on France's defeat, expected little more than a month's worth of campaigning and planned his wedding for August 2! General Friedrich Paulus himself, one of the brains behind Operation *Barbarossa*, thought that by the beginning of fall, the USSR would have been "mortally" wounded. This was a general consensus amongst the OKH. At the end of September, General Wagner, also from the OKH, was not worried about the Russian reserve deployed against *Typhoon*, because he considered

A panzer group was usually commanded by a *generaloberst* (colonel general). All four panzer groups—1st, 2nd, 3rd, and 4th—were deployed in support of Operation *Barbarossa*. They were vital to the *blitzkrieg* style of warfare. Command of a panzer group was a prestigious position. The place of these groups in the overall command structure was recognized in October 1941 when both 2nd and 1st Panzer Groups became panzer armies, with 3rd and 4th following suit on January 1, 1942.

Semyon Timoshenko commanded the Western Front during the summer of 1941, and led costly counteroffensives near Smolensk. He then took on various commands in the south of Russia, and did not play any role in *Typhoon*. The Germans however, still thought they were fighting Timoshenko's Army Group. (Ph. Rio Collection)

it was just "trash." Yet, Army Group Center's commanders were suffering from the stress and fatigue caused by extended campaigning, like Colonel General Maximilian von Weichs whose health deteriorated while he was in charge of the Second Panzer Army. Field Marshal Fedor von Bock, commander of Army Group Center and Colonel General Heinz Guderian of 2nd Panzer Group, did not get along, with Guderian reproaching von Bock for his lack of understanding of mobile warfare. Von Bock also had difficult relationships with other subordinates, like Colonel General Erich Hoepner, commander of 4th Panzer Group, and Field Marshal Günther von Kluge, commander of the Fourth Army. In addition the commanders of the panzer groups, like Guderian, did not get along with their colleagues who commanded the more "classic" armies. The later accused, sometimes with good reason, the panzer troops of neglecting their flanks and rear, which the infantry then struggled to protect, whilst the panzer troops felt the infantry were still stuck in 1918.

The troops and the officers on the ground did not necessarily share the optimism felt by the staff. On the eve of Operation *Typhoon*, Erich Kern, freshly arrived on the front, was talking with a veteran during guard duty:

A recurring scene of Army Group Center's advance in Russia during the summer: German columns coming across Soviet wrecks. Here a Luftwaffe car passes a BA-10 armored car. (Unknown photographer/ECPAD/Defense)

A Kfz 2 car drives through a burning Russian village. (Unknown photographer/ ECPAD/Defense)

The 3.7cm Pak 36 remained the standard antitank gun of the German Army and the Waffen-SS. Already inefficient in 1940 against the Char B1 bis and Matilda tanks, its obsolescence proved critical in 1941 when the Red Army brought in KVs and T-34s. (Heinrich Freytag/ECPAD/Defense)

"Look at the map of Russia. The country is huge. And where have we got to? Not even as far as Napoleon in 1812. Our conquest is just a thin strip of land on the map."

"But we have better technology and very different equipment from what they had!" I replied.

He gave a short laugh. "Sure but they are more prone to breaking down."[1]

---

1   D. Stahel, *Operation Typhoon*, pp.19–20.

An infantry column on the march. The soldiers carry large quantities of equipment including ammunition crates. Most German infantry on the Eastern Front were not supported by motorized transport.

Three military policemen, recognizable by their gorgets, seem to have just put up this sign warning of the presence of partisans, forbidding any vehicles to travel alone and ordering troops to keep their weapons within reach. In early fall 1941, "partisans" were mainly isolated *frontoviki* (front-line troops), as the resistance movement was still embryonic. (Bundesarchiv Bild 1011-007-2477-06)

The dusty roads, which became muddy with the first rains, lowered morale. The rugged tracks wore out the soles of the soldiers' boots so that by the end of the summer, there was a shortage in some units. Moreover, while the losses suffered remained bearable, some infantry divisions had already been forced to disband battalions, with several regiments reduced to only two. The battles of the summer around Smolensk, in which the Soviet artillery were able to use concentrated if rather imprecise firepower, played a significant role in this attrition. The Katyusha multiple rocket launcher was first used against Army Group Center on July 14, near Orsha. It is therefore not surprising that some began to have doubts. A non-commissioned officer of the 79th Infantry Division wrote on September 24: "I doubt that we will be done in Russia before the end of the year." But a lot of soldiers remained confident. On the same day, another soldier wrote: "Kiev is finished. Now the Center is back. The grand finale will be played in the east. We are placing all our hopes in the next four weeks."

Reinforcing Army Group Center

Both the front-line soldier and Bock had cause to be optimistic. The reinforced Army Group Center comprised six armies with 47 infantry divisions, six motorized divisions and 14 of the 21 existing panzer divisions. Resources originally allocated to Army Groups North and

This KV-2, claimed by the 12th Panzer Division, was put out of action during the fighting in the summer. There's no obvious damage, it may just have broken down, like more than half the tanks lost by the Red Army. (Unknown photographer/ECPAD/Defense)

Joseph Stalin managed to mobilize the country for a fight to the death against Nazi Germany, but made a series of catastrophic mistakes that allowed the German army to launch an apparently decisive offensive against Moscow at the end of September 1941.

South, as well as the Armored Reserve of the OKH were added to Army Group Center's initial components, which had already included nine panzer divisions. The 2nd and 5th Panzer Divisions were fresh, experienced and fully staffed after a period of recovery and maintenance following operations in the Balkans. There were also assault guns, a weapon which had no equivalent in the Red Army, which often compensated for the lack of anti-tank weapons, even if they struggled to destroy T-34s and KVs. There were no fewer than 14 Sturmgeschütz battalions available to Army Group Center when Operation *Typhoon* began. This represented a total of around 350 Sturmgeschütz IIIs, including the rare motorized units privileged enough to have a six-machine battery, like the famous Infantry Regiment Grossdeutschland that joined Operation *Typhoon* in early October. However, apart from a handful of powerful self-propelled guns—which incidentally were highly vulnerable—the only weapons able to overcome the newest Soviet tanks consisted of towed pieces and 5cm Pak 38s and 8.8cm Flak 18s, the latter heavy and slow to maneuver.

The Luftwaffe added its weight to the operation—Luftflotte 2 was allocated two groups of Bf 110s specialized in ground attack. Added to this were three groups of Bf 109 fighters and a squadron of Spanish pilots, the Escuadrila Azul—the Blue Squadron—an airborne version of the volunteer division deployed at the same time with Army Group North. The total figures were dizzying. *Typhoon* mobilized almost two million soldiers, 14,000 artillery pieces, more than 1,000 panzers and nearly 1,400 aircraft—although when the offensive started only 548 fighter planes were operational, including reinforcements. But the Luftwaffe was confident: since July 15, the highest-scoring ace, Werner Mölders, had accrued over 100 victories, and others were nearing that score. Some felt that in the sky too, the Russians could only deploy "trash."

The Red Army: Adapt or Die

If the Reich's difficulties during *Barbarossa* seemed to mainly comprise simple delays, for its part the USSR seemed to be fighting for its very survival. The Soviet leadership were under no illusion that the aim of the German invasion was anything less than the annihilation of the "Workers' Homeland" or rather, according to the Nazi terminology, the "Judeo-Bolshevik threat." After an initial slow response to the launch of *Barbarossa*, the country

Army Group Center Logistics

Logistics were the Achilles heel of Army Group Center, possibly even of the Ostheer. On July 14, while fighting was raging near Smolensk, General Wagner, responsible for the OKH's logistics, adjusted his estimates. Whilst just the day before he had estimated he could resupply Army Group Center's panzer groups all the way to Moscow, he now recognized that they would need to stop in Smolensk, the infantry being unable to go further than the Dnieper. The Red Army's counteroffensives then slowed the advance of Army Group Centre who quickly used up their supplies, especially munitions, preventing the build-up of stocks and the maintenance of the panzers. This pause did however give the logistic services a modest break, especially welcome to those in charge of train transports, which were already overwhelmed by their task.

On the eve of *Typhoon*, the logistics situation was still not satisfactory. The conversion or re-use of the Russian rail network had been delayed and Army Group Center was receiving 12–20 trains a day, rather than the 30 it needed. Army Group Center was receiving on average one tank for eight lost, and only sufficient spare parts to repair half of those requiring maintenance. With 30–40 percent of non-armored vehicles out of service, the recovery of captured trucks was vital. At least half of the initial fleet came from the spoils of the 1939–40 campaigns, leading to a nightmarish hunt for spare parts. The situation became so critical that in September, the Führer agreed to send Army Group Center 300 tanks, 350 tank engines and 3,500 trucks for *Typhoon*. The Luftwaffe was facing similar shortages. The situation was not as bad for the infantry; the troops were living in part off the country—plundering local resources was part of the *Barbarossa* plan.

Army Group Center decided to prioritize the supply of ammunition over the delivery of winter clothing stocked in Poland—an understandable choice as they expected to defeat the USSR before the end of the year. The Germans had to be optimistic because supplies were still not reaching them, even as the offensive was beginning. Admittedly, Army Group Center now benefited from four rail terminals far into the USSR, but it then had to make use of motorized columns already worn out by the local road network and lacking in fuel—the panzer divisions had only about half what they needed for an offensive operation.

In short Army Group Center could only rely on two-thirds of the 13,000 tons of supplies it required. The three transport groups of the Luftflotte 2 could only supply 200 tons—a drop in the ocean. The further the troops advanced, the more delivery of supplies diminished. It was therefore with quite a handicap that Army Group Center started Operation *Typhoon*.

Moscow was protected by significant antiaircraft batteries, as shown by this 76.2mm M1938 air defense gun. It was at that time the standard piece, but would be progressively replaced by the even more efficient 85mm. In any case the Luftwaffe failed to conduct any efficient raids against the capital. Its meager resources were required for direct support of the *Typhoon* troops.

adapted radically to the threat. The motivation came from Stalin, who on July 3, in a famous radio speech, called the Soviet citizens, not only "comrades" and "citizens" but also "brothers and sisters." The dictator understood that he could not mobilize his empire simply by playing the socialist card, and that he needed to stimulate a more patriotic feeling: the war would become known as the "Great Patriotic War." The official newspaper of the Communist Party, *Pravda* (*The Truth*), used this expression on the front page of its June 23 edition. In his speech Stalin also reminded his audience that "history shows that there is no invincible army and that there never has been," quoting clearly the example of Napoleon Bonaparte—would 1941 yet echo 1812?

The loss of Russian materiel between June and September had been astronomical: 20,000 of the 24,000 tanks on the Red Army's inventory; 14,000 aircraft, of which 1,500 had been destroyed on the ground on the first day of the offensive; and more than 25,500 Soviet guns were recorded in German warehouses on December 20. By the end of September, 100 infantry divisions had disappeared. The first convoy of supplies from the United Kingdom arrived on October 11, but the volume was small. At the start of the fall, the USSR asked the United Kingdom for 1,100 tanks per month, but only 4,800 were supplied for the whole of 1941. The USSR had to rely on its own resources.

Moving factories in the west further east meant the country could fight a long war, with its industry out of the enemy's reach, but it caused problems in the short term, with the production of armor falling to its lowest level in the conflict—160 KVs, 170 T-34s and 320 lighter models came out of the factories in October, often leaving the new tank brigades understaffed and ill-equipped. This monthly total of 650 tanks should however be put in perspective. The Third Reich built fewer than 4,000 tanks and assault guns in 1941. The KV and T-34 tanks only represented 10 percent of the armor on Ivan Konev's Western Front. The situation was the same for aircraft and other weaponry. New models were a long time in coming, like the PPSh-41 submachine gun and antitank rifles. These existed, but not their bullets! In addition relocating factories limited the Red Army's strategic mobility at a crucial point with 60 percent of the railroads' capacity allocated to the transfer of factory machinery—in October 500 companies and more than 200,000 laborers left Moscow.

The Red Army needed to adapt radically. As early as the end of July, it adopted lighter allocation tables. Rifle divisions lost their heavy artillery, a third of their numbers, half their machine guns, two-thirds of their antitank guns, two-thirds of their 82mm mortars, etc. This new allocation, while more realistic, was still difficult to achieve. Indeed, only 7,200 field artillery pieces came out of the factories in 1941. Between June and July 55 divisions were formed, and brigades were formed in September. These "half" divisions could be created in a few weeks, sometimes less, and 159 of them were in existence by the end of the

A Ju 88 in Sverdlov Square, Moscow. This reconnaissance unit aircraft, of 122 Reconnaissance Group, was shot down at the end of July. The Luftwaffe's blitz against the capital took place mainly between July 21 and August 22. Afterwards, losses and limited resources restricted their attacks to nuisance raids. The Soviet Air Forces—Voyenno-Vozdushnye Sily (VVS)—launched similar operations against Berlin until September.

year. In addition there was the volunteer militia, with 23 divisions in Leningrad and Moscow in July alone. The cavalry and air force also adopted lighter allocations. Cavalry divisional numbers were 60 percent lower, and they had no tanks. Fifty of these divisions were formed during the summer. Air regiments went from 60 to 30 aircraft and all efforts were focused on providing direct support to the troops. The navy in turn formed "navy infantry brigades" and a myriad of smaller detachments for a total of 150,000 men by the end of 1941.

These spectacular reforms allowed the Red Army to deploy new forces by the summer, though not without cost. Army corps disappeared on July 15, due to lack of sufficient staff personnel, and the Fronts now had smaller armies than their German counterparts. Nevertheless, 28 armies appeared between July and September. The country's mobilization system proved very efficient, ensuring a continuous flow of new recruits and formations for the committed armies: 5.3 million reservists were called up in June, 3.5 million would be added to that by the end of the year, not counting the volunteers. In short, without taking into account about 100 divisions coming from other regions of the USSR, nearly 200 were put in place in 1941, twice what the Germans had estimated. Such mind-numbing figures explain how the Red Army managed to deploy such massive numbers in September, to face Army Group Center on Moscow's doorstep.

A War of Annihilation

While hundreds of thousands of Soviet citizens did collaborate with the invader, the Ostheer's crusade of unheard-of violence meant that many more would voluntarily enroll to fight it. The criminal orders of the Nazi regime—including the infamous Commissar Order— were widely followed, despite later denials by German generals. Communists, especially political commissars, and Jews, to be followed by the entire population, were destined for extermination. Einsatzgruppe B carried out this mission at the rear of Army Group Center and by mid-November claimed to have killed at least 45,000 Jews. Furthermore, Halder, Chief of Staff, declared that "the troops must participate in this ideological battle until the end of the eastern campaign." Crimes against civilians would not to be prosecuted. In this statement he was only following Hitler in his *Vernichtungskrieg* (war of annihilation).

If the Führer intended to spare the military by entrusting the mass killings to the Einsatzgruppen and some SS units, he had not created enough of them. Across the whole front there were only 3,000 men in the Einsatzgruppen and 11,000 of Himmler's Kommandostab Reichsführer-SS, although they worked solely for Army Group Center. And so, by the time of the first massacres at the end of June, police and soldiers were often assisting. Information on these massacres and the brutality of the invaders soon reached the rest of the country, and contributed in motivating the *frontoviki*, who understood that this war was a fight to the death. There was plenty of courage in the Red Army's ranks; in fact, several divisions earned—the hard way—the honorary title "Russian Guard" during the fighting around Yelnya.

However, morale was still fragile. Defeat followed defeat, and the Red Army was constantly giving ground. And if the violence of the Nazis soon became apparent, many citizens were more afraid of their own regime's. As early as June 22, desertions and volunteer

The Front West of Moscow, 30 September 1941

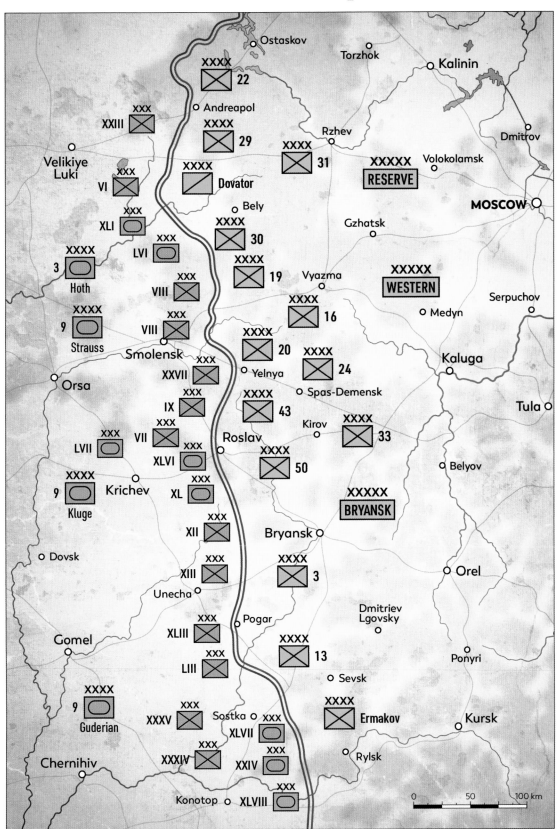

surrenders multiplied. In any case a missing soldier, or even a prisoner, was considered a deserter. The People's Commissariat for Internal Affairs (NKVD) were kept busy behind the front lines, preventing desertions through a rule of terror. The fear of "traitors" remained though, and in August, Balts, Ukrainians, and Belarusians were forbidden to serve in tank crews. Boris Ponomarenko, head of the Belarusian Communist Party—and future leader of the Partisan Movement—underlined in a letter to Stalin on September 3, that "the retreat has caused a blind panic." It was definitely not for lack of a brutal discipline: from mid-July, some high-ranking officers criticized the abuse of the death penalty at a time when losses in combat were already so high. Some cases were staggering. A lieutenant shot three soldiers—one of them a woman—who came to his unit without an officer, asking for food.

Soviet riflemen were commonly known as *frontoviki* (which means infantry fighting at the front). All able-bodied Russian men were eligible for conscription at the age of 19. During the Great Patriotic War, most *frontoviki* were in their twenties, and had grown up knowing only the Soviet system. Before the war training lasted six months, but necessity shortened it to just a few weeks.

The Red Army was also suffering from a lack of equipment and training. For example, the Moscow Militia's 5th Division, created in July, was without 50 percent of its weapons, and was partly armed with Polish rifles. One regiment only had half of its machine guns and rifles, of which several were obsolete models, and no mortars, infantry or antitank guns. On September 26, without any further provisions beyond a change in uniforms, the unit became the 113th Rifle Division within the Reserve Front's 33rd Army.

The Soviets also lacked means of communication. Radios were few and far between, impeding the artillery's efficiency, who had difficulty coordinating or even directing fire, or adapting to a fluid situation, such as a tank breakthrough. To make matters worse, the Red Army—to the delight of the enemy—did not protect its transmissions very well.

A *frontovik* pledges allegiance by kissing his Mosin-Nagant M1938 rifle.

The Stalinist purges and the initial disasters of the war had created a shortage of officers at all levels, which resulted in some swift promotions. Only three of the 15 army commanders in charge of defending Moscow had held that command on June 22. Six had been named in August, most of them having previously only commanded corps or divisions. Five came from the NKVD, having the advantage, according to Stalin, of being trustworthy and firm. In contrast to the German staff, personal grudges and tensions seem to have been generally absent between the Soviet commanders. Furthermore, Soviet generals were usually younger by five to ten years than their German counterparts, which proved an asset in the fierce struggle to come. On the downside, their experience was on occasion limited, another consequence of the purges of the late 1930s. Georgy Zhukov, who would come to play such an important role in the following weeks, described the new commander of the Reserve Front's 24th Army, Major General Konstantin Rakutin: "I had never met Rakutin. His situation report impressed me, but it was obvious that his training in tactics and operations was inadequate. He obviously suffered from the same disadvantages common to the officers and generals of the NKVD; he had had no opportunity to develop his knowledge of operational art."

Several of the generals defending Moscow were not lacking in skills and were on a different level altogether. Ivan Konev and Andrey Eremenko, commanding the Western and the Bryansk Fronts respectively, were competent but had to work with forces suffering from the issues mentioned earlier. Some of their subordinates were also future rising stars of the Red Army, such as Konstantin Rokossovsky, then at the head of the Western Front's 16th Army; but he had only just arrived and had never before been in command of more than an improvised army corps.

Just like the German 5cm leGrW 36, in 1941 the 50mm Soviet mortar was the standard indirect support weapon for a company. This is an RM-38, later improved on, until it was replaced by the RM-41 model.

The last great weakness of the Red Army lay in its evaluation of the situation. The Kiev disaster had been an enormous surprise, as the Soviets had initially thought that the enemy's main objective was Moscow, which explains the relentlessness with which they launched counteroffensives in Yelnya and around Smolensk. The Western Front was prioritized for reinforcements. In the aftermath of the battle for Kiev, on September 26, Stalin thought it was too late in the year for an effort against Moscow and refused to take into account the information provided by his intelligence services. He therefore decided to send reinforcements first the south and then Leningrad. Furthermore, it was not until September 10, that the Western and Bryansk Fronts went into defensive mode, worn out by futile assaults against Army Group Center. The last offensive launched by the Bryansk Front, September 2–6, resulted in 100,000 losses. Tank units and motorized troops were especially weakened, but the Soviets retained an offensive position. Dovator's Cavalry Group, combining cavalry and tanks, held a sector against German infantry. Moverover, Stalin refused to listen to any advice about mobile defenses. The artillery—mostly horse-drawn—was also positioned close to the front. The positioning of the forces was also clumsy, the Reserve Front's 24th and 43rd Armies being placed on the front line between two other Fronts. To make matters worse, fortifications were incomplete. Although construction had started in early July, the two lines defending the capital were still not finished—less than half of the planned lines were complete by the time *Typhoon* started, and a large proportion remained unoccupied. Finally, the intelligence was defective. Army Group Center was thought incapable of attacking, with preparations for *Typhoon* and moving panzers not reported. In contrast, the Germans had a fairly good picture of the opposing forces, especially of the lines between the various fronts, always a weak point.

It is not surprising then that the offensive came as a real shock to the Soviets when, on September 30, Heinz Guderian struck.

These antiaircraft artillerymen remain vigilant behind their quadruple Maxim. This weapon was inefficient against bombers, unless they were flying at low altitude, but even then it did not always cause fatal damage.

In Profile:
Semyon Budyonny 1883–1973

Born into a poor peasant family, Semyon Budyonny was drafted into the Imperial Russian Army in 1903, becoming a cavalryman. During World War I he received the St George Cross several times for acts of courage. He organized a cavalry force when the Civil War broke out in 1917, which eventually became the 1st Cavalry Army, the *Konarmiya*, and which helped the Bolsheviks to victory. Budyonny joined the Bolshevik party and formed a close bond with Stalin. In 1935 he was made one of the first five Marshals of the Soviet Union. Three of the five were killed in the purges, but as he had Stalin's full support he escaped.

Budyonny was a brave and colorful cavalryman but he never shone as a strategist or military thinker and refused to admit that tanks could replace his beloved horses. Nevertheless, in 1941 he was made commander-in-chief of the Southwestern Front. Dismissed and replaced by Timoshenko in September he was then given command of the Reserve Front. He had the dubious honor of being the general with the largest number of disasters during the war. However his status as a Civil War hero kept him safe, and he survived the war, being allowed to retire as a Hero of the Soviet Union.

A Typhoon between Vyazma and Bryansk

Operation *Typhoon* officially began on October 2, but Guderian's 2nd Panzer Group started to advance on September 30. Unfortunately for the Ostheer, it was the most exhausted and least well-supplied armored group.

In September, Hitler and the OKH had originally planned *Typhoon* with only the 3rd and 4th Panzer Groups, who were charged with forming a huge *kessel* (pocket) around Vyazma. Bock altered the plan to include Guderian's panzer group, at that time engaged in the Kiev battle, but whose inclusion allowed the encirclement of the Soviet armies around Bryansk, and therefore the reduction of those forces defending Moscow. The details of how to take the capital did not hold much interest, and thus while the attackers had a good picture of the enemy's front-line units, they knew nothing of his reserves. Guderian, given the distance he would need to cover, and the fact that he wanted to secure the communications crossroads of Orel, east of Bryansk, started his advance on September 30. 2nd Panzer Group formed

Close-up shot of two Panzer IIIs, 11th Panzer Division, in a burning village. The nearer panzer displays both the division's insignias, the ghost and the circle crossed by a vertical line. (Heinrich Freytag/ECPAD/Defense)

A *frontovik* has paid the ultimate price defending the Motherland. The Soviet fortifications were well conceived, but not elaborate enough to stop the panzers in *Typhoon*. (Heinrich Freytag/ECPAD/Defense)

the southern arm of the pincer movement intended to trap the Bryansk Front. With its 16 extra divisions, nine of them mechanized, *Typhoon* became the largest offensive since Operation *Barbarossa*, not only because of its strategic importance, but also because of the resources committed and size of the theater of operations: more than 600km from north to south. However, it differed from the June offensive in that it had just one objective. Meanwhile, the Red Army was anticipating a break after the fighting around Smolensk. Its awakening was all the more brutal because of it.

On September 30, the weather in Glukhov, north of Konotop, was abysmal. An armored army assembled behind 15th Machine Gun Battalion, vanguard of XXIV Panzer Corps. The advance of the tracked and untracked vehicles, all marked with a "G" for Guderian, took place in torrential rain, which quickly turned the ground into a bog. Trucks, motorbikes, even some tracked vehicles, struggled. Moreover, not all elements of 2nd Panzer Group had arrived. Meanwhile, the whole of XLVIII Panzer Corps was on alert on the southern flank, threatened by clumsy Soviet attacks. Covering the northern flank was the responsibility of the 1st Cavalry Division, the only one in the Heer, which was stretched out across 60km up to the Second Army. Luckily, it was a marshy area at the edge of the famous Pripet. The operations around Kiev, only recently concluded, had put a strain on the men, who had only had a few days to rest after a 200km march. Consequently, on the 27th, the four panzer divisions were limited to 187 operational panzers, including 94 Panzer IIIs, and 36 Panzer IVs, with 149 more Panzer IVs due to arrive soon, but after the beginning of *Typhoon*. As for human losses, less than half the 32,000 casualties had been replaced. More importantly

A few KV-2s saw action during *Typhoon*. No longer in production, most had been lost during the summer campaign. Some, like this one pictured here, were put back into service by the Germans. (Unknown photographer, Champigné Collection/ECPAD/ Defense)

though, the logistics situation was dire. There was only enough fuel to move 200km when Moscow was over 500km away and Orel 250km. Worse still, the railway terminal where the panzer group drew its supplies, was in Konotop, 80km away from its starting point, whilst other elements of Army Group Center were sometimes 20km from the front line.

The Stukas Attack

The initial success, which exploited the element of surprise on a unwary enemy, was nonetheless total. Guderian entrusted his *schwerpunkt* (main focus) towards Orel to the XXIV Panzer Corps, helped in the north by the XLVII Panzer Corps, and in the southeast by the XLVIII Panzer Corps as a flank guard. The XXIV Panzer Corps of General Baron Geyr von Scheppenburg involved the 3rd and 4th Panzer Divisions, part of which fought as a *kampfgruppe* under Colonel Heinrich Eberbach. Built around 35th Panzer Regiment, this *kampfgruppe* also included elements from the 3rd Panzer Division spearheaded the offensive (see box on page 60). From 06:00, a powerful artillery barrage, lasting 30 minutes and including two heavy 21cm howitzers, pummeled the Russian lines. Despite the overcast weather, the Stukas (*Sturzkampfflugzeug*, dive bombers) took aim at Ermakov's group, then barring the road to Orel with his infantry at the front, cavalry behind, and with two tank brigades in reserve. But on this relatively open ground, their defensive strategy was not optimal, the *frontoviki* having undergone several weeks of futile and costly offensives. These formations, incomplete and badly equipped, saw themselves facing a mass of panzers operating with unparalleled efficiency. The 283rd Division yielded under the assault. The

A Pkw Horch 830R, from Guderian's 2nd Panzer Group, leading a convoy of trucks. This was the beginning of *Typhoon*, and as the bad weather had not yet struck, the road was still usable. (Speck/ECPAD/Defense)

Two Ju 87 B-2s of Stab (staff) II/StG 1, returning from a mission. *Typhoon* took advantage of the inclusion of StG 2 and part of the StG 77, sent from other sectors of the front. (Unknown photographer/ECPAD/Defense)

riflemen lacked antitank weapons, apart from Molotov cocktails, which they could only use when the panzers were almost on top of them. The Red Army therefore had to come up with desperate measures to stop the panzers.

Antitank Dogs

The 3rd Panzer Division was covering the left of the 4th Panzer Division with Kampfgruppe Manteuffel, including a mechanized infantry battalion and an artillery group. They easily overpowered the *frontoviki* until they came to a village where the defenders were putting up a stout resistance. The first elements stopped in the center of the village, when suddenly some dogs came bounding up, aiming for the half-tracks, ignoring the machine-gun fire: "Obergefreiter Müller cried out 'It's got something on its back!' His colleagues identified a wooden lever about 25cm long. It rose vertically from a rack on the dog's body. A few Russians had jumped up from their positions in the trenches, encouraging the dogs on." The Germans shot seven of these "mine dogs," then radioed in news on this new danger. Having played their last card, the defenders left the village, but the Germans then fell prey to a heavy artillery bombardment, including Katyusha rockets. The rockets would prove to be much more efficient against tanks than dogs.

Close-up shot of an SdKfz 10/4 opening fire on an unthreatening target, judging by the lack of precautions taken by the men, and apparently the photographer too. This vehicle belonged to the Luftwaffe (registration WL) who supplied most of the Wehrmacht's antiaircraft units. Note also the woolen greatcoats, necessary as the temperatures quickly dropped from September. (Heinrich Freytag/ECPAD/Defense)

Kampfgruppe Eberbach (4th Panzer Division), September 30, 1941

Staff, 5th Panzer Brigade (Colonel Heinrich Eberbach)

Panzers

35th Panzer Regiment (110 tanks on September 26, 100 (?) on September 30)

2nd Battalion, 6th Panzer Regiment (see box page 39)

Infantry

34th Motorcycle Battalion (4th Panzer Division, three rifle companies, one machine-gun company and one heavy company—pioneer, antitank guns and infantry)

3rd Motorcycle Battalion (*idem*, provided by the 3rd Panzer Division)

Artillery

2nd Battalion, 103rd Artillery Regiment (10.5cm howitzers)

1st Battalion, 53rd Nebelwerfer Regiment (15cm multiple rocket launchers)

2nd Battery, 60th Artillery Regiment (10.5cm K18 guns)

Engineers

79th Pioneer Battalion (4th Panzer Division, minus one company)

3rd Company, 39th Pioneer Battalion (3rd Panzer Division)

79th Bridge Company (4th Panzer Division)

Antitank Defenses

3rd Company from 49th Tank Destroyer Battalion (Antitank guns battery, 3.7 and 5cm pieces)

Antiaircraft Defenses

2nd and 5th Battalions of 11th Anti-Aircraft Regiment (heavy and light batteries, 8.8 and 2cm pieces)

A Panzer 35(t) supporting some *schützen* during a fight in the undergrowth. Two of the seven infantrymen have MP40 machine pistols instead of their Mauser Kar 98K rifles. The excellent MG34 machine gun meant that the individual German infantryman's firepower was easily superior to his opponent's. (Bundesarchiv)

This close-up view of a Pak 36 underlines the advantage of this small antitank gun—its maneuverability. It could also fire explosive shells, and thus support the infantry. (Heinrich Freytag/ECPAD/Defense)

Meanwhile, Kampfgruppe Eberbach made easy progress towards its first objective, Sevsk, and at around 08:00 it came across the tanks of the 150th Brigade near the village of Essman, with only 20 tanks—eight light T-50s and 12 T-34s. The former did not pose much of a threat to the Panzer IIIs who destroyed three of them without incurring a loss. However, two T-34s were waiting for them in a very good position, covering a mined corridor under the rubble of a railroad embankment. Immediately, Eberbach sent a Panzer III company to take the T-34s on their flank, but to no avail, losing a tank instead. In the meantime, a few Bf 110s had arrived and engaged the T-34s despite the antiaircraft fire. Colonel Boris Bakharov, seeing the damage, ordered the remnants of the brigade to fall back. Meanwhile, Colonel Nikolai Radkevich, an experienced commander with his 121st Brigade and 70 tanks (including six KV-1s and 18 T-34s) in a good position on Kampfgruppe Eberbach's flank, did not attack. And so Guderian's main force was allowed to continue. To the north, the XLVII Panzer Corps met with similar success opposite the weak and poorly trained 298th Division. However, this time, the 141st Tank Brigade counterattacked with its KV-1s and KV-2s. The Germans then deployed their 88s and 10.5cm pieces. The rain of steel destroyed two KVs and forced the others to retreat. Worse still, the Russian commanders drew the wrong conclusions about Guderian's objectives. Indeed, Ermakov informed Eremenko, whose HQ was in Bryansk, that he was only being attacked by one armored corps, which his superior, worried about movements on its west flank, took to be a diversion. He thus ordered Ermakov to deal with the problem on his own.

On October 1, Kampfgruppe Eberbach took Svesk at around 11:00, assisted by a Stuka bombardment. It easily overcame the few defenses, and took control of the bridges across the eponymous river, leaving them intact. It also captured two aircraft in full working order on the airfield. At the same time, the vanguard seized the heights north of the town and captured 17 heavy howitzers. When a counterattack finally came—probably the 121st Brigade—the panzers, artillery and antitank guns had had time to take up defensive positions. Advancing in small groups of three to six tanks, the Soviets were subjected to a deluge of shells, which forced them to flee east. In short, Ermakov completely failed to stop Guderian. A section of the Kampfgruppe Eberbach actually left towards the end of the afternoon, and by nightfall had seized Dmitrovsk, 100km away from Orel. The German advance proceeded apace—without meeting any opposition—through a swamp area, via two bridges, that had also been left intact. Despite this favorable terrain, Ermakov had taken no measures to bar Eberbach's way. In Dmitrovsk, the Germans seized some considerable booty, such as vehicles delivered by the British, such as several American Jeeps.[1]

The following day Eberbach's advance continued, but this time with a *Vorausabteilung* (advanced guard). Fuel was already becoming a problem for the whole *kampfgruppe*, spread as it was between Svesk and Dmitrovsk with the muddy roads delaying the supply trucks. However the delay was not significant and by 13:45 they arrived at Kromy, the last step before Orel. A Soviet warehouse taken on the way was a pleasant surprise and the resistance encountered remained symbolic.

1   Information taken from the regimental diary of the 4th Panzer Division, published by a former officer of the division, p.305.

Few Soviet photographs were actually taken at the front and this one is probably no exception, despite its realism.

Paras to the Rescue

It was however a different story in the air: three regiments of biplane fighters, Polikarpov I-153s and Petlyakov Pe-3s, attacked the columns of the 4th Panzer Division with bombs, guns and rockets. They claimed 30 trucks and 33 tanks, though these numbers are exaggerated. The Bf 109s were too "short-legged" to cover the sector and only the anti-aircraft guns could protect the panzers, which they did quite effectively. The raids, led by a hundred or so of these machines, were the first sign of the beginning of a Soviet response, though on the ground Ermakov was still inactive. Indeed Kromy's defenders were caught digging their fortifications and the Germans apparently even called Orel, 50km away, to assure the local authorities that there were no panzers in town! The Russians reacted slowly and paid dearly for their initial lethargy. However, Eremenko was starting to take a better measure of the threat; he had sent the VVS to attack Guderian's columns and even asked for reinforcement from the Stavka (Soviet High Command). But Stalin was more preoccupied by the situation in Ukraine and in Leningrad. He promised to send two divisions of riflemen and two tank brigades to Orel for "October the 3rd or 4th." A little more original and dynamic, at dawn on the 3rd, the air force sent from Moscow the 201st Paratrooper Brigade, followed by the 10th, directly to Orel's aerodrome. But it was too late.

Eberbach's main worry was once again supplies and thus at 11:00 on the 3rd, he was only able to send part of his *kampfgruppe* towards Orel: 35th Panzer Regiment, a motorcyclist battalion, a motorized infantry battalion, and several artillery batteries. This time, not only were they targeted by the VVS, but a bridge on the Oka river was blown up in front of the

A panzer company, more of a support company, moving through a village, its *isbas* bearing the scars of war. *Barbarossa* forced the Germans to put the Panzer IV into the primary role, the Panzer III proving inferior to the T-34 and KV. (Jacobsen/ECPAD/ Defense)

An SdKfz 253 and an SdKfz 10 (which used the same chassis but was not armored). The former was used for artillery observation and was quite rare. Some Sturmgeschütz battalions were equipped with it. (Heinrich Freytag/ECPAD/Defense)

The I-16 was still common in the Soviet Air Force, like this type 17, characterized by its two ShVAK 20mm guns that afforded it considerable firepower. It was a formidable opponent for the Bf 109s, whose pilots used their speed to counter its maneuverability. When the battle for Moscow began, this small plane made way for more modern models. (G. Gorokhoff Collection)

panzers, that lost a few machines there; a ford allowed the motorcyclists to cross while the pioneers repaired the bridge. The Germans then approached the town's main aerodrome, which they bombarded with artillery. Some panzers might even have shot at some of the cumbersome four-engined TB-3 transport places, which the paratroopers were hurrying to disembark from after their landing. The motorcyclist battalion barged into the air base under cover of antiaircraft gunfire. The Russian paratroopers had few heavy weapons,[2] apart from some howitzers and antitank guns, but managed to set fire to two tanks with Molotov cocktails. Owing to the panzers' presence, the last battalion of the 201st consequently diverted to another landing ground, north of Orel. The 10th Brigade did the same, but losing several TB-3s and PS-84s (the Russian equivalent to a DC-3) to German fighters, which had finally arrived. At the air base German firepower made the difference, even if the panzers had to shake off aggressive paratroopers by throwing grenades at them from their turrets. Although the Germans took 400 prisoners, part of the 201st Brigade managed to escape northwards. The Germans lost several panzer commanders, shot in the head by snipers. This tough engagement continued until nightfall. It was not the last time that the Soviet paratroopers would shine in combat.

In the meantime, at around 17:15, First Lieutenant Arthur Wollschlager's 6th Company, 35th Panzer Regiment, rushed ahead into Orel, alone, disobeying orders to hold the town's west approaches, and it proved a lucky decision. He surprised an antitank battalion on the move—shooting or even crushing enemy troops before they could react. His few tanks then went on to take several bridges and the Orel train station, without suffering any losses. Wollschlager quite literally crossed the town without any reaction from the military or

---

2   The paratroopers' regulation rifle was the SVT-38 or 40 semi-automatic, which gave them more firepower over light weapons.

An I-16 Type 18 prepares take off. This version was usually armed with four 7.62mm machine guns, but this one is armed with rockets, sometimes used—without much success—in aerial combat. The I-16 was nicknamed *Ishak* (donkey) by the Russian pilots due to a similarity in pronunciation. (G. Gorokhoff Collection)

German soldiers inspect a TB-3 four-engined aircraft, a bomber dating back to the early 1930s, but widely used during the war. It was however limited to nocturnal flights and predominantly used for transporting and dropping paratroops. These aircraft transported the 201st Brigade of the 5th Airborne Corps to Orel. (Speck/ECPAD/Defense)

civilians. A tram even rang its bell when its path was blocked by a Panzer III, which it had mistaken for a Russian tank. The gunner is then said to have aimed his barrel in front of the tram, causing the passengers to flee. Journalist Vassili Grossman did not notice anything amiss until one of his colleagues came running to him: "The Germans are in Orel. They have hundreds of tanks. I miraculously escaped the gunfire. We must leave now or they'll get us!"[3] However, while Wollschlager had only half a dozen tanks, at around 19:00, he was joined by motorcyclists and the motorized infantry. Wollschlager would receive the *Ritterkreuz* (Knight's Cross) for his audacity at Orel.

Taking this large town—an important transport hub with 120,000 inhabitants—so easily was a great success for Guderian. His men had advanced 250km in four days. The rest of 2nd Panzer Group also met with success, though perhaps not on quite as spectacular a scale. Indeed the threat of the XLVII Panzer Corps made Eremenko move the 13th Army north, which opened the way northeast for the panzers who were trying to close the pocket. While Eberbach entered Orel, Lemelsen's forces cut the road between Orel and Bryansk. As Eremenko waited for the panzers south of Bryansk, the latter positioned themselves to strike east. 2nd Panzer Group was repeating its June accomplishments: a fast and decisive advance against inefficient opposition, suffering only limited losses compared to the enemy. As of

---

3   V. Grossman was a correspondent for *Krasnaya Zvezda* (*Red Star*), the armed forces' daily newspaper.

In Profile:
7th Panzer Division

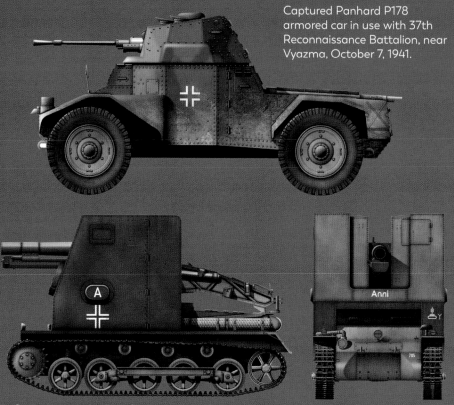

Captured Panhard P178 armored car in use with 37th Reconnaissance Battalion, near Vyazma, October 7, 1941.

15cm sIG 33 auf Panzer I (Sd.kfz 101), 705th Self-propelled Heavy Infantry Gun Company, assigned to 7th Panzer Division, northwest of Vyazma, October 10, 1941.

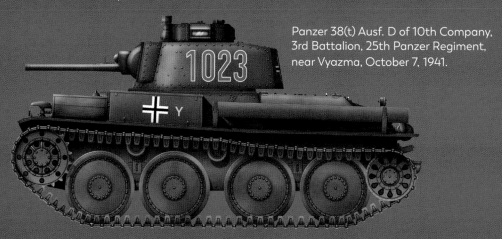

Panzer 38(t) Ausf. D of 10th Company, 3rd Battalion, 25th Panzer Regiment, near Vyazma, October 7, 1941.

The small and vulnerable command vehicle Panzerbefehlswagen I was still widely used at the beginning of *Barbarossa*, but in theory, only at battalion or regimental level. The last Panzer Is in service were often used for spares for the PzBefw Is. (Heinrich Freytag/ECPAD/Defense)

September 30, the 4th Panzer Division had lost 41 men killed, 120 wounded, six Panzer IIIs and IVs destroyed, against 1,500 prisoners, 50 guns, 16 tanks and 400 captured vehicles. The material losses were mostly largely compensated, the 3rd Panzer Division receiving 35 new tanks. 2nd Panzer Group was already talking of 10,000 prisoners, and more importantly had perfectly fulfilled its role in Operation *Typhoon*.

General von Weichs, with glasses, commander of Second Army, watches as a Panzer IV Ausf. E, from 6th Panzer Regiment, 3rd Panzer Division, passes. The future Field Marshal Model's division played a small role in the first week of *Typhoon*, generally in the shadow of the 4th Panzer Division, mostly due to logistics problems.

The Decisive Battle

Typhoon officially started on October 2. Two panzer groups and three infantry armies began the offensive, turning Ermakov's mishaps into an overall catastrophe for the three Fronts defending Moscow. Was Hitler's final victory against "Judeo-Bolshevism" finally coming to pass?

During the night of October 1/2, Army Group Center officers read to their troops—at least those not on the front lines—a letter from the Führer:

> Soldiers! Today the main, final and decisive battle of the year begins. It will lead to the defeat of the enemy who is facing us, as well as the instigator of this war—England. By neutralizing the enemy in the east, we will eliminate England's last ally on the continent, and a terrible threat for the German Reich and the rest of Europe, a threat of a type unknown since the time of the Huns and the Mongols. The thoughts of the German people will be with you in the following weeks, even more so than before.
>
> We already owe you so much, for everything you and our allies have achieved. The German people are with you because, with the help of God, you will give the Fatherland, not only victory, but also the most important prize of peace.

A Panzer III crosses a ford, far from the front, judging by the protective gun covers. The vast majority of the Panzer IIIs engaged in *Typhoon* possessed a 5cm KwK 38 gun, which could easily pierce the armor of most Soviet tanks, with the meaningful exceptions of the KV and T-34. (Heinrich Freytag/ECPAD/Defense)

A Soviet staff officer sets a good example to his men digging trenches. The Red Army paid dearly for its insufficient fortifications when *Typhoon* began. (Ph. Rio Collection)

This is a prime example of Nazi rhetoric, radically inversing responsibility for the conflict, as well as the aggressive nature of the regime, which—according to Hitler—was only defending itself. Whether it was just optimistic propaganda speech or not, it is true that the main offensive started very auspiciously. Indeed, Army Group Center—now attacking an enemy on full alert— took advantage of the threat Guderian posed to Timoshenko's Army Group's southern flank. Moreover, the favorable weather was helping crucial air support, and the road network was now negotiable. So, at 05:30, the front lit up with the preparatory bombardment. The Luftwaffe flew 672 missions that day, and nearly a thousand the next day, bombing artillery positions, command posts, and enemy columns. According to plan, the 3rd and 4th Panzer Groups advanced while the infantry armies limited themselves to either supporting attacks, or diversions, waiting for the Soviets to be weakened by the panzers. The Second Army was tasked with disrupting the Bryansk Front, which was trying to stop the advance of Guderian's 2nd Panzer Group. But whilst the two armies formed a pocket around Bryansk, *Typhoon*'s main force targeted the Western Front, in the shape of a gigantic pincer closing on Vyazma.

Hoepner vs. Budyonny: 4th Panzer Group's Fantastic Ride

Unfortunately for Stalin's faithful servant, the 4th Panzer Group was the most powerful German armored group. Colonel General Erich Hoepner's three motorized army corps comprised no fewer than six panzer divisions and two motorized divisions, including the SS-Das Reich, and not forgetting several independent armored groups, like the Sturmgeschütze battalions. Additionally, the 2nd and 5th Panzer Divisions, both fresh and strong, were also part of the 4th Panzer Group. Overall, a mass of 765 tanks swept over the Soviets on October 2, aiming for Spas-Demensk, 50km away, the first objective.

Facing it was the 43rd Army of Semyon Budyonny's Reserve Front, comprised of four poorly equipped divisions and two tank brigades covering 85km. The 43rd Army had some advantages, like the proximity of the Desna river, woodland terrain, and some advanced fortifications. However, they were disadvantaged by the state of their weaponry, particularly antitank weapons: the divisions had only one third of the 45mm antitank guns that a pre-war division would have had—18 rather than 54.

Sturmgeschütz battalions were self-propelled assault gun detachments, part of the artillery branch and not units of the infantry divisions.

Hoepner's main force included the XL Panzer Corps and the XLVI Panzer Corps, on a 25km front. The LVII Panzer Corps, which was waiting for several dozen new panzers, remained in reserve. After a storm of Nebelwerfer rockets, General Stumme unleashed the two armored divisions of his XL Panzer Corps. If the first Soviet Katyusha rockets terrified the German infantry, the Nebelwerfer rockets proved to be just as efficient on Russian trenches and bunkers. And whilst they were not too accurate, that was not the case with the Stukas, who eliminated at least one artillery battery. Consequently, the infantry easily crossed the Desna, and by 08:00, the bridge company was hard at work as the advance continued. An undamaged bridge across a parallel watercourse was taken by 09:00. Elsewhere the panzers of the 11th

German soldiers using the Panzerbüsche 39 antitank rifle, which only worked against the lighter Soviet tanks. In contrast the Soviet antitank rifles coming into service at the end of 1941 would prove more formidable, even if they did not destroy that many panzers. (Bundesarchiv Bild 101I-283-0619-31)

Order of Battle: Red Army Defending Moscow (September 30, 1941)

WESTERN FRONT (Lieutenant General Konev)

16th Army (Major General Rokossovsky):
38th, 108th, 112th, 241st and 127th Rifle Divisions; 127th Tank Brigade (71 tanks)

20th Army (Lieutenant General Ershakov):
73rd, 129th, 144th and 229th Rifle Divisions

29th Army (Lieutenant General Maslennikov):
178th, 243rd, 246th and 252nd Rifle Divisions

Dovator's Cavalry Group (Major General Dovator):
45th, 50th and 53rd Cavalry Divisions; 101st and 107th Mechanized Divisions; 126th, 128th and 143rd Tank Brigades

19th Army (Lieutenant General Lukin):
50th, 89th, 91st, 166th and 244th Rifle Divisions

22nd Army (Major General Yushkevich):
126th, 133rd, 174th, 179th, 186th and 256th Rifle Divisions

30th Army (Major General Khomenko):
162nd, 242nd, 350th and 251st Rifle Divisions.
Total of 486 tanks for the Front.

BRYANSK FRONT (Lieutenant General Eremenko)

3rd Army (Major General Kreizer):
137th, 148th, 269th, 280th and 282th Rifle Divisions; 4th Cavalry Division

50th Army (Major General Petrov)
217th, 258th, 260th, 278th, 279th, 290th and 299th Rifle Divisions; 108th Tank Division (around 100 tanks)

Front Reserves:
7th Guards Rifle Division; 154th and 287th Rifle Divisions; 42nd Tank Brigade

13th Army (Lieutenant General Gorodniansky):
6th, 121st, 132nd, 143rd, 155th, 298th and 307th Rifle Divisions; 55th Cavalry Division; 141st Tank Brigade (25 tanks)

Ermakov Group (Major General Ermakov)
2nd Rifle Division of the Guard; 160th and 283rd Rifle Divisions; 21st Mountain Cavalry Division; 52nd Cavalry Division; 121st and 150th Tank Brigades (54 tanks; 20 tanks)
Total of 257 tanks for the Front.

RESERVE FRONT (Marshal Budyonny)

Front line:

24th Army (Major General Rakutin)
19th, 103rd, 106th, 139th, 160th, 170th and 309th Rifle Divisions; 144th and 146th Tank Brigades (90 tanks for the army)

Second line:

31st Army (Major General Dalmatov)
5th, 110th, 119th, 247th and 249th Rifle Divisions

33rd Army (Major General Onuprienko)
17th, 18th, 60th, 113th and 173rd Rifle Divisions

43th Army (Major General Sobennikov)
53rd, 149th, 211th and 222nd Rifle Divisions; 145th and 148th Tank Brigades

32th Army (Major General Vishnevsky)
2nd, 8th, 29th and 140th Rifle Divisions

49th Army (Lieutenant General Zakharkin)
194th, 220th, 248th and 303rd Rifle Divisions; 29th and 31st Cavalry Divisions.

Front Reserves: 147th Tank Brigade; total of 301 tanks for the Front.

SOVIET AIR FORCES (Voyenno-Vozdushnye Sily (VVS))

18 fighter regiments: 12 bomber regiments, and 7 ground attack regiments: a total of 946 aircraft, of which 545 operational (301 bombers, 201 fighters, 13 Il-2 Shturmoviks and 30 reconnaissance aircraft.

Note: There were several battalions of 20 to 30 tanks, in theory meant to accompany the infantry, or more rarely the cavalry.

These two fighters illustrate perfectly the reality of the Soviet formations developed in haste after the summer of 1941—lacking uniform and armed with a motley assortment of weapons. The man on the left seems to be carrying a Polish wz.30 light machine gun, seized in 1939. (RIA Novosti)

Panzer Division, XLVI Panzer Corps, simply crossed the Desna at a ford, the defenders not having placed mines there. The element of surprise was no longer present, yet the successes of Guderian's panzer group seemed to be building momentum.

Budyonny had not planned a true in-depth defense, and the Germans easily pushed past the weak divisions of the 33rd and 43rd armies, who paid a high price for their lack of experience. The ex-militia soldiers of the 113th Division, 33rd Army wasted their bullets at the first sight of a German soldier, whilst others were already panicking. With no antitank guns, they unsuccessfully resorted to using Molotov cocktails against the panzers. The division had the rare privilege of having a Katyusha rocket battery, but its imprecise firing failed to stop the enemy, or even to inflict significant losses. In the end some survivors were forced to surrender, but the rest managed to flee, meaning that the 113th Division escaped total destruction. The tanks of the 2nd Panzer Division sometimes reported surprising Soviet artillerymen while they were setting up their batteries. The two tank brigades of the 43rd Army were defending Spas-Demensk. Budyonny, on an inspection, barely managed to escape with his life as the Germans advanced. The ease with which 4th Panzer Group had pushed past almost two full Soviet armies, seemed to vindicate the OKH's and Army Group Center commanders' judgment of the Soviet reserves.

His first objective met, Hoepner continued with his advance towards Vyazma on October 5, the LVII Panzer Corps now in the van.

A crew from the 108th Tank Division photographed next to their KV-1 "Ekramanni," whose armor is reinforced with bolted plates. This extra weight did not improve the reliability of these giants, and the division failed to stop the panzers.

A Soviet column has been surprised whilst retreating. The gun visible on the left is a perfect example of the 7.62cm 1936 F-22, here towed by an S-65, out of proportion to the weight of the piece. (Heinrich Freytag/ECPAD/Defense)

Members of 689th Propaganda Company preparing for work. Note the Berliner bear insignia that identifies this small unit as being attached to the Fourth Army. Each panzer group/army had its own propaganda company. The result is a large pool of photographs, which explains in part the prominence of German pictures in publications on the Eastern Front. (Unknown photographer/ECPAD/Defense)

3rd Panzer Group's Attack

At the outset of the operation 3rd Panzer Group was commanded by Colonel General Hermann Hoth, until he was replaced on the 5th by Georg-Hans Reinhardt. The advance comprised only three panzer divisions, two of which came from Army Group North; and like 2nd Panzer Group, there were logistics problems. Furthermore, Army Group North, which had just barely arrived in the area, had had no time to undertake maintenance. The 6th Panzer Division's main combat tank was the Panzer 35(t), acquired from Czechoslovakia's defunct army, and considered obsolete since March. The reliability of these worn-out machines was becoming more and more of an issue and a lack of spare parts meant that some machines had to be cannibalized to repair others. In total, 3rd Panzer Group only had 400 panzers against Konev's nearly 500 tanks, whose Western Front also benefited from woodland, hilly terrain and good fortifications, none of which was favorable to large motorized formations.

Konev was in fact the general who had best prepared his troops for an in-depth defense, with significant reserves. Two pre-war armies would face the panzers, including the 91st which had arrived from Siberia in August. In contrast with the formations hastily raised in July, they fielded a significant arsenal in theory. However the panzers struck at the junction between the 19th Army and 30th Army, which was still suffering from the heavy losses—up to as much as 50 percent—inflicted during the pointless summer offensives against Army Group Center. As a result of this there were on average only three antitank guns for every

Operation *Typhoon* saw its share of river crossings against strong currents, especially on the Desna. Nevertheless these soldiers are clearly not under fire. These inflatable boats are capable of transporting more than a ton, so the 400kg Pak 36 was not an issue. (Wilhem Voigt/ECPAD/Defense)

This maze of signs is typical of the Wehrmacht. Note the insignia at the top that resembles that of the 7th Panzer Division, a "Y." (Unknown photographer/ECPAD/Defense)

kilometer. To make matters worse, half of Konev's tanks were in Dovator's Cavalry Group, facing the Ninth Army, while the rest were scattered elsewhere.

The results of Hoth's offensive is reminiscent of Hoepner's successes in the south. His artillery comprised the new Nebelwerfer rocket launchers, which proved more significant to the outcome of encounters in 1941 than the Russian equivalent. His two army corps synchronized an attack on a 10km front and broke through the 91st and 162nd Divisions without any difficulties. The former had fought the 7th Panzer Division with some success in August, but this time the 6th and 7th Panzer Divisions of the LVI Panzer Corps combined their strength and formed Panzer Brigade Koll, a little like Guderian's Kampfgruppe Eberbach. These 300 machines overwhelmed the opposition—on the first day, Colonel Richard Koll reached his objectives and captured more than 500 prisoners, at the price of two killed and eight wounded. And at the same time, the infantry secured the flanks. Some *landsers* (German infantrymen) discovered to their great surprise and delight that the Russians had already supplied their encampments with warm winter clothing—daytime temperatures barely reached 50°F.

The next morning, a *kampfgruppe* from 6th Panzer Division seized two intact bridges over the Dnieper in Kholm-Zhirkovsky, in the district of Smolensk, whilst Konev tried to counter the panzers. Unfortunately, his artillery could not follow the pace, and the first counteroffensive, launched by a tank brigade, mistakenly attacked the German infantry. In the end Konev's defenses, no matter how elaborate—antitank trenches, obstacles, buried tanks, etc.—were unable to stop Hoth's *kampfgruppes*. The Soviet general then launched a counterattack with tanks from Dovator's Group against Hoth's bridgehead on the Dnieper. It was a job for General Ivan Boldin and his group, the 101st Motorized Division, 152nd

Even for tracked vehicles and in good weather, the USSR terrain was often difficult. Here, a Panzer IV lends a hand to another. Amongst other things, the Ostheer lacked powerful towing engines. (Heinrich Freytag/ECPAD/Defense)

A Soviet artillery unit has clearly been caught whilst being moved. The discarded rifles testify to a rather limited resistance. (Heinrich Freytag/ECPAD/Defense)

As was to be expected, the Red Army tried to destroy all road structures, to delay the enemy's progress. Here, pioneers have built an improvised bridge onto the remains of the old one. The driver of this Pkw SdKfz 2 is maneuvering with extreme caution. (Unknown photographer/ECPAD/Defense)

and 166th Rifle Divisions, 126th and 128th Tank Brigades. The general had at his disposal a large force of some 190 tanks, including around 20 T-34s and KVs, accompanied by infantry and artillery. On October 4, Boldin engaged both his rifle divisions on the left wing and his tanks on the right, by the southeast, against Kholm-Zhirkovsky's bridgehead. A detachment of the 129th Infantry Division held the sector, quickly rejoined by Colonel Erhard Raus's *kampfgruppe*, from the 6th Panzer Division, who described the battle:

> One hundred tanks were coming by the south, towards the crossroads at Kholm. Most of them were only medium tanks (BTs and T-26s) against which I sent just one Panzer 35(t) battalion and 6th [Mechanized] Company, 114th Schützen Regiment. This meager force was enough to contain this potentially dangerous threat, until the antiaircraft and the antitank guns could be organized in an adequate antitank security line between Kholm and the Dnieper bridge. Their tanks, scattered in small groups because of the forest, never managed to organize a powerful and unified armored breakthrough. Their forward elements were taken out one by one, as they met the antitank positions. Consequently, the Russian commanding officer became more and more careful and spread out his vehicles across the battlefield in such a way that the next tank attacks, all done separately and in small numbers, were all dealt with by our antitank guns and pulverized…

Raus's testimony reminds us how the panzers reacted to enemy tank attacks—by letting the artillery take care of the tanks, if they were KVs and T-34s. It also shows that it was not

The Panzer III of page 40 arrives on the other side of the river and climbs up with no apparent difficulty. Note the track links reinforcing the frontal armor. (Heinrich Freytag/ECPAD/Defense)

Panzers II follow the Panzer III. No markings or insignia can be seen. Contrary to the Panzer III, this small tank was less and less useful at the front. It was even too slow for the reconnaissance missions that they were sometimes sent on. (Heinrich Freytag/ ECPAD/Defense)

enough to bring together tanks and infantry to obtain a cohesive joint task force. Indeed Boldin failed to coordinate his troops, the riflemen had not followed the tanks, more than half of them being left behind. Once these clumsy assaults had been dealt with, the Koll Brigade even succeeded in intercepting most of the enemy's artillery.

The two rifle divisions did not meet with any more success against 129th Infantry Division. The counteroffensive that Konev had planned ended in dismal failure. However, contrary to the tone of Raus's testimony, the panzers did suffer heavy losses—28, plus three Sdkfz 251s were left on the battlefield, plus 11 Panzer 35(t)s that broke down. The lack of German equipment was starting to tell.

Hoth now faced a different, though not unexpected, problem: the lack of fuel. While Boldin's counterattacks did persist on the 5th—with even less success than the day before—it was above all, logistical deficiencies stopping the advance of the 7th Panzer Division. With the 6th Panzer Division it was meant to lead the LVI Panzer Corps advance towards Vyazma, 60km away. Due to a lack of aircraft, the Luftwaffe could only parachute in sufficient fuel for a *kampfgruppe* of the 7th Division, entrusted to Colonel Hass von Manteuffel. This colonel still had his 25th Panzer Regiment and one motorized regiment, though he had to wait until 14:30 before moving on, which forced him to carry on after nightfall. However, these issues did not seem to overly worry the Germans. On October 5, General Wagner, supposedly in charge of the logistics at the OKH and presumably aware of the issues facing Army Group Center noted that: "The operational objectives being set would previously have made our hair stand on end. East towards Moscow! Then I think the war will be almost over, and

The crew of this Pak 38, from the 11th Panzer Division—see the ghost insignia on the right-hand mudguard—have unfolded the canvas top of their SdKfz 10 to avoid the rain. (Heinrich Freytag/ECPAD/Defense)

perhaps the [Soviet] system will crumble… I am constantly astonished by the Führer's military judgment. He intervenes in operations, it could be said most decisively, and up to now has always been right."

Indeed, events would seem to prove Hitler right, as the largest encirclement of the war unfolded.

The 10.5cm leFH18 howitzer was the standard artillery piece of the German army, each infantry division having 36 pieces. At 3.5 tons it was heavy and therefore not entirely suitable to a war of movement, but it fired antitank shells, an important asset in 1941. The leFH 18 would remain in service until the end of the conflict. (Lüthge/ECPAD/Defense)

The Encirclement of Vyazma and Bryansk

Only with *Typhoon*'s main assault did Stalin and the Stavka begin to realize the danger that threatened Moscow. Was it too late? For the soldiers surrounded between Vyazma and Bryansk, it certainly seemed so.

When Guderian launched 2nd Panzer Group towards Orel, the Stavka did not fully comprehend the threat and on October 1, Stalin even ordered Budyonny to send his 49th Army south to defend Kharkov and Kursk. Even as the first to be targeted by the German advance, Eremenko only reacted on the 1st, when aerial reconnaissance alerted him to

This damaged KV-1 has been abandoned in Mtsensk. It belonged to Colonel Katukov's 4th Brigade, one of the first formations to reinforce Moscow's defense.

Russian women digging an antitank trench on the Mozhaysk Line. Work began in the summer but had to be hurried when *Typhoon* started. Around 27,000 civilians—the great majority women, the elderly and teenagers—were mobilized in October. However, the line was still not finished by the time the panzers arrived.

the lines of panzers driving towards Bryansk and Orel. Moreover he misunderstood the intentions of Lemelsen's XLVII Panzer Corps, which was approaching Bryansk from the east rather than the south. In any case, orders often reached the rifle divisions too late; they were not overly mobile and were therefore incapable of countering the German armored formations, who were taking advantage of the roads while they were still usable.

Even though they immediately gauged the threat, both Budyonny and Konev failed to stop the panzers. The latter did attempt to launch a coordinated counterattack in contrast to Budyonny, who was unable to think of anything else but a static defense. Once the German infantry forces joined the offensive, the Soviet riflemen were pressured on all sides. The Red Army staff also paid the price for its inexperience and its deficient communications, as the pincers quickly closed around Bryansk and Vyazma.

Stalin—who like his subordinates suffered from fragmentary and delayed intelligence—initially ordered his forces to hold at all costs, thereby helping the panzers achieve their objectives. On the 5th, he had to admit that disaster was imminent, the three Fronts were nearly surrounded, and there were almost no other troops between the Germans and Moscow. The dictator then authorized Konev to have his Western Front fall back, but lost contact halfway through the conversation.

The only sector with a force capable of stopping the Germans was in the south. Stalin had charged General Dmitry Lelyushenko, a competent officer, with taking command of the 1st Guards Rifle Corps, and charged him to form a corps in two days and stop Guderian's

"Defend Moscow!" cries the *frontovik* on this poster, brandishing a semi-automatic rifle SVT-40 in front of the Kremlin. For the Russians, the capital's defense brought back memories of other tragic moments in their history, like the threats from Poland, Sweden and France. (Ph. Rio Collection)

An avenue in Moscow bristling with an impressive array of obstacles and barricades. As with Leningrad, Hitler decided very early on to lay siege and starve the city rather than take it by force. However, he still had a long way to go. (Ph. Rio Collection)

Some sectors on the Mozhaysk Line posed formidable obstacles for Army Group Center. This road has been very effectively blocked with steel Czech "hedgehogs."

This pig crossing the path of tanks from the Gespenter Division (Ghost Division), might well end up under the knife. Far from simply adding to the variety of their rations, pillaging for food was part of the German strategy during the USSR invasion. The population was to be reduced by starvation. (Heinrich Freytag/ECPAD/Defense)

advance in the area of Orel. The arrival of its components was delayed due to various crises, but on the 4th, the general was in Mtsensk, 50km northeast of Orel, and the trains transporting Colonel Mikhail Katukov's 4th Tank Brigade were arriving. Lelyushenko also joined an NKVD regiment to his cause, and the paratroopers from 5th Airborne Corps, parts of which had already engaged with the 4th Panzer Division. Whilst he realized he could not push back the enemy, he readied himself to resist mercilessly.

The Pincers Close

As these preparations were being made, the battle on the main front was increasing in intensity. Indeed, three days after the official launch of *Typhoon*, the three Army Group Center infantry armies were engaged in combat. In the north, the Ninth Army first had to protect the flanks of a weakened 3rd Panzer Group. From October 3, it covered the flank north of Hoth, blocked the 16th Army and infiltrated an army corps between the 16th and the 19th armies. The 16th Army was unable to respond, for instance with its tank brigade, and to confront the panzers that were destroying its neighbor. The infantry was also cleaning up behind the panzer group, surrounding for example, the remains of the 91st Division before it could escape. A similar situation could be observed further south, where von

This Schützenpanzerwagen is a commander's SdKfz 251/6—note the loop antennae—modified to transport six Wurfgerät rockets on the sides. These are absent but the mounts are clearly visible. This vehicle belonged to the 11th Panzer Division, whose ghost insignia can just be seen. The photograph may have been taken during the Kiev fighting, which would explain the "K" of Panzer Group Kleist, 1st Panzer Group. (Heinrich Freytag/ECPAD/Defense)

Kluge's Fourth Army did not see action until October 4. Despite having inferior numbers against an alert and well-entrenched opponent, the Fourth Army launched an exemplary attack. The artillery preparation and the following assault smashed through the riflemen of the 20th and 24th armies around Yelnya, a kind of revenge for the humiliating retreat in early September. Once again the Germans exploited an incongruity of the Soviet strategy—the two armies were from the Western Front and the Reserve Front respectively. The 144th Brigade of the 24th Army counterattacked without success when its T-34s came up against Paks and Sturmeschütz. Whilst it was an undeniable success for the Fourth Army, Konev had not made it easy. On the 5th, the 191st Sturmeschütz Battalion reported that it had lost 15 machines, though some of them were probably repairable. Two German generals had been killed, the commander of IX Army Corps and a divisional general.

Finally, Colonel General von Weichs's Second Army acted to draw the attention of the Bryansk Front. Convinced, despite all the signs, that the main attack would come from the west, Eremenko underestimated the danger posed by Guderian and it was against the Second Army "threatening" Bryansk that he would send his 108th Tank Division. In short, his only true mobile reserve, with 40 T-34s and KVs, dozens of light tanks, two infantry and motorized artillery regiments, and support units was wasted against the Second Army rather than being deployed to block Lemelsen's panzers. Weichs perfectly succeeded in his mission, with no excessive losses.

A column of Sturmgeschütz—assault guns—takes a break on a muddy road, typical of the Russian road network in the fall of 1941. Note the half-tracks SdKfz 252 and 253, the first transporting munitions, the second command and observation gear. Not all Sturmgeschütze batteries and groups benefited from these. (Bundesarchiv 1011-140-1212-04A)

The Panzers of *Typhoon*

The panzers used during *Typhoon* in early October 1941 did not differ from the ones deployed at the beginning of *Barbarossa*. The panzer divisions still mostly deployed Panzer IIIs and IVs, the latter for fighting against Russian tanks and the former for support missions. While tactics were adapted to the Soviet operational theater, the doctrine for panzer use remained the same. Indeed, from Białystok to Kiev, success awaited the Panzer troops, who more than ever considered themselves the Wehrmacht's elite, and the ones to win the war. However, as soon as they came up against T-34s and KVs they began to realize that their panzers were not all they had thought them to be—their weapons, armor, and even mobility, were inferior—especially in comparison to the T-34. However, despite alarming reports, neither the high command nor the engineers paid much attention to the Soviet tanks. The 8.8cm antiaircraft gun was generally considered to be sufficient to deal with the threat. It is true that the Russian tanks did suffer from multiple faults—bad ergonomics, poor reliability, mediocre optics—and were badly used in small groups in suicidal attacks, by often poorly trained crew.

German armored weaponry had other weaknesses, with all but the 2nd and 5th Panzer Divisions starting the offensive in a state of exhaustion. Four panzer divisions also used Czech tanks—the Panzer 35(t) and Panzer 38(t)—less powerful than the Panzer III. All of them still had Panzer IIs in their ranks, or even a few Panzer Is, vulnerable against even the lightest of Soviet tanks. Overall, even if there were sufficient numbers of panzers, a solution to the armored beasts they were facing had to be found. Several divisions—the 4th, 17th and 18th amongst others—chose to spread out their heavy towed pieces, sometimes a 10.5cm howitzer battery, but more often one or two 8.8cm antiaircraft guns, or 10.5cm K18 artillery. The latter two were especially heavy and slow to deploy, however they could pierce any enemy armor, even from a long distance.

Sometimes more original solutions were adopted. Despite supply issues, the 6th Panzer Regiment of the 3rd Panzer Division managed to maintain three panzer battalions with three companies. The first had 17 Panzer IIIs, the second five to six Panzer IVs—half the theoretical quota—while the third was actually the 521st Antitank Battalion, attached to the division. Its nine small self-propelled 4.7cm guns were poor compensation for the lack of Panzer IIIs. Nevertheless, even when the division received 35 new Panzer IIIs and IVs, it maintained a group of Panzerjäger Is in each panzer battalion.

It is interesting that no panzer unit seems to have repaired captured T-34s or KVs. While they did not lend themselves well to the war of movement the Germans still intended to lead, this oversight is still surprising. In August Army Group Center did create its first Beutepanzer (captured tanks) units, but they were put to use by security divisions at the rear. The Panzer troops kept faith in their equipment, because in the Soviet forces the T-34s and KVs were far outnumbered by older more vulnerable tanks. The three fronts defending Moscow had just 128 T-34s and 47 KVs out of the 849 tanks deployed. Even then they were scattered in the armies with no bulk for the maneuver reserve. It is perhaps not surprising that these few machines, powerful as they were, were not a concern to powerful joint task forces such as panzer divisions.

A PaK 38 antitank gun, towed by an SdKfz 10, which means it belonged to a mechanized division, the infantry often having to make do with captured tractors. PaK 38s were rarely seen in more than one platoon per antitank company, and were conspicuous by their absence in some divisions. (Jacobsen/ECPAD/Defense)

A gigantic cauldron was being formed, surrounding most of Timoshenko's army group. To the south, Lemelsen's XLVII Panzer Corps, although not quite as spectacular in its results as von Schweppenburg's XXXIV Panzer Corps in Orel, widened the breach between the 13th Army and the Ermakov Group, already expanded by Eremenko's orders. Lemelsen's main push was made east of Bryansk. The Soviet general did order the 141st Brigade to stop the panzers at Karachev, but what could 25 tanks do against two panzer divisions? On this occasion the 18th Panzer Division reported "mine dogs," though with no more success than expierenced against the 3rd Panzer Division. And so on October 6, a small *kampfgruppe* led by Major Hans Gradl entered Bryansk by the Karachev road without meeting any resistance. Eremenko discovered that the Germans had arrived when the panzers started firing on his headquarters. Eremenko, though wounded, did manage to esacpe. Gradl and his small detachment, just like First Lieutenant Wollschlager in Orel, secured Bryansk even before reinforcements arrived from the 17th Panzer Division. A stock of 10,000 Molotov cocktails, 17 tanks, 22 guns and a thousand prisoners fell into German hands. They took a town of nearly 90,000 inhabitants with nearly no losses. Eremenko's Front was not under any command, its staff having fled northeast, and Lemelsen had just isolated 14 rifle divisions.

It was the same near Vyazma. On October 6, Reinhardt, who had just succeeded Hoth as the head of 4th Panzer Group, launched elements of the 7th Panzer Division east. The 24-hour delay was due to fuel shortage, but that did not seem to disturb Kampfgruppe Manteuffel, 25th Panzer Regiment and 6th Schützen Regiment. Despite the strength of the advance, its objective was to close up the pocket and avoid any major engagement. The Panhard armored cars of the reconnaissance group guided Manteuffel, and sometimes drove past retreating

The Red Army abandoned guns, tractors and carts during the retreat. The piece in the foreground is a 152mm ML-20 howitzer. This excellent materiel would probably have been re-used by the Germans. (Speck/ECPAD/Defense)

Prisoners, some perhaps crew from the abandoned vehicles in the background, leave for Nazi camps. Their attention seems to be caught by the German soldier on the right, who is searching the battlefield. (Heinrich Freytag/ECPAD/Defense)

Russian columns. The *kampfgruppe* did not really meet with any opposition; Konev was trying in vain to maintain a coherent front. He ordered a retreat towards Vyazma that came to naught: at 17:00 Manteuffel's vanguard reported that they had reached the Moscow–Vyazma road, 2km north of Vyazma. Most of the 7th Panzer Division had only just received the fuel allowing it to move But nevertheless, the 4th Panzer Group, despite its deficiencies, despite the enemy's defenses and Konev's counterattacks, had fulfilled its objective.

As for 3rd Panzer Group, the LVI Panzer Corps had led the way since Spas-Demensk was taken, helped by the 10th Panzer Division. The latter also sent a *kampfgruppe* to take Yukhnov, on the Ugra river, stepping-stone to Moscow some 200km away. Budyonny and the Stavka both seemed to be out of their depth. The crew of a light Pe-2 bomber reported that the panzer columns advancing on the road from Warsaw to Moscow came up against limited resistance. Nevertheless the panzers did have some problems. The 10th Panzer Division suffered from a shortage of fuel, with muddy fords on a tributary of the Ugra river, east of Yukhnov, and from the attentions of the VVS. Raids by the I-153 and R-5 biplanes and the more modern Il-2s and Pe-2s harassed the division and destroyed a bridge. But the Luftwaffe kept watch: ace Gordon Gollob claimed two Pe-2s, his 52nd and 53rd victories, the Soviet regiment losing four bombers. Temperatures continued to drop, and during the night of the 6th, the first snow fell. The *landsers* were struck by the beautiful white coat that

These Moscow artillerymen at a PVO (antiaircraft defense) aim their quadruple Maxim machine gun up to the skies. This was the principal light Soviet antiaircraft weapon in 1941, used on trucks as well as armored trains. The concept was excellent and would be used again after the war with weapons that performed better than the M1910. (RIA Novosti)

covered the countryside, but they soon came to resent it when the panzers got stuck in a deep, sticky mud. The 10th Panzer Division still managed to send a *kampfgruppe* towards Vyazma. On the 7th, due to a lack of gasoline, only one squad of panzers left as a vanguard, but as usual still managed to take the defenders by surprise. At 06:00, it had seized the bridges south of the town. Most of the 2nd Battalion, 7th Panzer Regiment followed an hour later and crossed Vyazma with no opposition. The militia and the few antiaircraft pieces defending the city were no match. The panzers then received the order to take care of the river bridge north of the town. At around 09:00, they observed gray-colored vehicles guarding the bridge. Recognizing Panzer 38(t)s, they fired blank rockets, and the Panzer 38(t) replied in kind. The 10th Panzer Division had linked up with the 7th Panzer Division, which was just sealing the Vyazma pocket. At the same moment, the two divisions from the LVII Panzer Corps positioned themselves facing west, to prevent any of the troops they had surrounded from escaping. More than 700,000 Russian soldiers were trapped.

The Last Fires?

The Stavka and Stalin finally grasped the full meaning of the German victory. In the space of a few hours they went from incredulity, to mild worry to near panic. With Yukhnov's fall Stalin understood how close the enemy was to his nearly defenseless capital. Up until now the density of the three fronts rendered the presence of significant reserves west of Moscow unnecessary; but now they were on their way to being destroyed by *Typhoon*. On the ground, the full scale of the catastrophe was revealed, especially as confusion took hold. The best example is given by the account of General Konstantin Rokossovsky of the 16th Army and his staff. Sent from the Western Front, they left their divisions to the care of the 20th Army, a measure that seemed so absurd to the general that he first asked for confirmation. Rokossovsky however, was told to find in Vyazma five divisions and with his "new 16th Army" launch a counterattack towards Yukhnov. On the 6th, a conference was organized in the crypt of Vyazma cathedral with the officers present. But there were no units in Vyazma, only militia. Rokossovsky was dumbfounded: "How is this possible? [...] I was assured that there would be at least five divisions awaiting here, ready to be attached to the 16th Army?" The meeting was cut short by the town's mayor barging in shouting: "The German tanks are in town!" Skeptical, Rokossovsky, replied: "Says who?" The official assured them he had seen them himself from the bell tower, so the officers climbed the tower and saw for themselves the panzers of 7th Panzer Regiment in the streets, firing on the cars they met. Just like Eremenko and Budyonny before him, Rokossovsky and his staff just managed to escape.

Panic rose as much in the rear as it did on some sectors of the front, although the people in Moscow were still unaware of anything amiss. On the 4th, Vassili Grossman, who had just escaped Eberbach's panzers in Orel, described the roads north of the town in this way:

> I thought I had already seen a retreat, but I had never seen what I was witnessing now, and I could never have imagined anything of the kind. An exodus! The exodus from the bible! Vehicles were advancing in eight ranks, theirs was the violent thundering of dozens of trucks simultaneously trying to get their wheels free of the mud. Huge herds of sheep and cattle were being led through the fields. They were followed by lines of horse-drawn carts, there were thousands of carts

In Profile:
Soviet Tanks

T-50, 150th Tank Brigade,
Essmann, September 30, 1941.

T-26, 1933 Model, 108th
Tank Division, near Bryansk,
October 5, 1941.

T-34, 1941 Model, 4th Tank
Brigade, Mtsensk, October 6, 1941.

An impressive column of new T-60s. In 1941, 1,818 T-60s were built, the ease of their production being one of the rare advantages of this poorly armed and poorly armored tank. (G. Gorokhov Collection)

> covered with colorful sacks, planks, tin objects… There were crowds of people on foot with bags, bales, suitcases. It was not a flow, it was not a river, it was the slow motion of an ocean's tide. A tide several hundreds of meters wide… There are times where I feel just as if we had been carried back to the era of biblical catastrophes.

This rather apocalyptic image corresponds to the Nazis' evaluation of the situation: "The enemy is broken and will not rise again," declared the German radio, quoting Hitler.

Indeed, by October 4, much of Army Group Center, the OKH and of course Hitler, were exulting in their success. Stalin's orders for a defense with no retreat had favored Operation *Typhoon*. Convinced of the battle's outcome, the Führer not only gave unrealistic objectives to Guderian despite his dire resupply issues, but wanted to push Army Group North in an ultimate effort to the south of Lake Ladoga, to ensure a total blockade of Leningrad. Concerns about the weather disappeared. The forecast of the day for central Russia was "sunny weather, almost summer temperatures." General Wagner's enthusiasm is not surprising. Goebbels wrote in his journal: "[…] maybe the weather god, who these last few months has not often favored us, has finally seen the light and will now, in these final and decisive weeks, be on our side."

Sealing the *kessel* on October 6 and 7 only served to reinforce this optimism. The destruction of Timoshenko's Army Group was progressing well. Only the Mozhaysk Line, the last and incomplete fortified line before Moscow, could stop the panzers.

The lack of significant troops in the Stavka Reserve (RVGK)—worried General Boris Shaposhnikov, the Stavka's excellent Chief of Staff. He could only allocate a handful of tank brigades and divisions to Lelyushenko when Guderian threatened Orel. Even then, they did not all come from the capital or the surrounding area, where the railway network was being mobilized for the convoys emptying the factories. Consequently, Katukov's 4th Tank Brigade, which arrived in Mtsensk on October 4, actually came from Stalingrad. On its way to Moscow, it was diverted just in time. The other formations did not arrive before the 5th, or even the 6th. These difficulties probably explain the absurd transfer of Rokossovsky and his staff to Vyazma without a combat unit. Some divisions were still in training—at least five rifle brigades from the province of Orel had been evacuated towards the Volga province to finish their training—and a new reserve army group was building up, but immediate resources were lacking.

The Mozhaysk Line was a set of four lines of fortifications protecting the western approaches to Moscow. It had been started on July 16 and was due to be finished on November 25.

In this state of emergency every day mattered. The Stavka asked again for the far-eastern armies, but again, the transfer took time. A few divisions were on their way, amongst them the 32nd, which left for Moscow at the end of September. In total, the RGVK fielded 14 rifle divisions and 16 tank brigades. Also mobilized were NKVD resources, as well as the militias and given the urgency, military schools. The latter enabled the formation of 42 brigades in October, including five around Moscow.

A medical corps detachment, including women, marches along a Moscow street towards the front in the early fall. Note the shell damage to the house on the left. (RIA Novosti)

Zhukov on left.

In Profile:
Georgy Zhukov

Born into a poverty-stricken peasant family, he was conscripted in the army in 1915. He was awarded the St George Cross twice and promoted for his bravery in battle. He joined the Bolshevik Party after the 1917 Revolution and fought in the Russian Civil War, serving with the 1st Cavalry Army. Based in the far east during the purges, Zhukov thus escaped Stalin's paranoia. During the summer of 1939, he organized a brilliant multi-task force operation against the Japanese army, that was severely beaten during the battle of Nomonhan/Khalkhyn Gol. Zhukov was declared a Hero of the Soviet Union. Transferred to the Stavka, he opposed Stalin in July 1941, which earned him a temporary disgrace, but his "skills" revealed themselves during his time in Leningrad. He sacrificed thousands of soldiers in costly, and probably pointless, assaults, as Hitler did not intend to take the city by force, but by starving it. Zhukov however, earned the image of a tough, but reliable and efficient commander.

In September 1941, the costly counterattack of the 24th Army, coordinated by Zhukov, pursued the Fourth Army out of the Yelnya salient and gave the USSR its first triumph in the conflict. On this occasion Zhukov regained Stalin's trust, and then went on to win more bloody "victories" that slowed the German advance towards Leningrad. He became the ideal man to defend Moscow.

Because of his role during the Great Patriotic War, he personally received the German Instrument of Surrender in 1945. Postwar he would become Minister of Defense and later a member of the Politburo.

But a leader was needed to bring this defense to life. Stalin first thought of Timoshenko, but on the 5th, decided on 45-year-old General Georgy Zhukov, then commanding the Leningrad Front. Delays and hazards meant that his aircraft did not reach Moscow before the 7th. At the Kremlin, Zhukov supposedly found Stalin rather somber, pessimistic and furious. He accused Konev of treason, based upon the temporary disruption of the communications with his headquarters, and the fact that he had asked for confirmation when Stalin demanded—wrongly—that his forces fight to the death. "Like Pavlov at the beginning of the war, Konev has opened the front to the enemy." The Vozhd (Stalin) was actually thinking about having Konev shot, just as Pavlov had been in July. Zhukov did not like Konev much—the feeling was mutual—but he needed Konev's knowledge and so defended his cause, earning Konev a reprieve. Boris Shaposhnikov then ordered Zhukov to go immediately to Konev's headquarters in Mozhaysk, and then to Budyonny's to take a measure of the situation. At this critical time for, his regime and his country, Stalin had just picked the perfect man.

This photograph of a Pak 36 in position in open terrain is clearly posed, but shows the compact appearance of the piece, which proved itself formidable against tanks such as the T-60. (Lüthge/ECPAD/Defense)

| Defending Moscow

Zhukov's arrival as commander of Moscow's defense did not immediately change the course of events. In fact the situation had never been more serious. The magnitude of the disaster between Bryansk and Vyazma was becoming apparent. But would Army Group Center be able to make the most of its advantage?

Zhukov's inspection showed him the fragility of the Soviet facilities in place in front of Moscow. He arrived in Mozhaysk in the evening of the 7th, where Konev, only just escaped from the Vyazma pocket, exposed the sad facts: a breach 500km wide with the panzers 200km away from Moscow, and less than 100km away from Mozhaysk. The 50th Division and the 18th Tank Brigade, freshly arrived that morning from near Moscow, were defending Gzhatsk (now Gagarin), the last important town before Mozhaysk. The Western Front commander was worried, as much by the strategic situation as by Stalin's mood; he feared that the latter wanted him executed, which Zhukov confirmed. Zhukov then had to find Budyonny. No one knew exactly where his headquarters were. Maloyaroslavets was mentioned, a small town southeast of Mozhaysk. Zhukov left in the middle of the night, in the snow on bad roads and in fear of meeting the German vanguard at any time. He managed

One of the interminable columns of prisoners photographed so abundantly by the propaganda companies during the fall of 1941. Over 1.2 million Russian prisoners were taken in the Kiev, Vyazma and Bryansk pockets. (Jacobsen/ECPAD/Defense)

A *frontovik* poses in front of his shelter. This anonymous soldier reminds us of the thousands of men who were lost in the Vyazma-Bryansk pockets, either killed on the battlefield or dead in captivity. (G. Gorokhoff Collection)

A group portrait of the staff of XLVIII Panzer Corps, 2nd Panzer Group. General Werner Kempf is third from the right. His army corps, which remained as reserve during the first phases of *Typhoon*, suffered from logistics issues and was slowed by the *rasputitsa* (muddy season) when the time came to move up the line. (Albert Otto/ ECPAD/Defense)

A 15cm sIG33 auf Panzer I (Sf), of the 702nd Heavy Infanteriegeschütz Company (motorized), is able to travel Russian tracks quite well. The company was attached to the 1st Panzer Division. Originally intended to destroy fortified positions, it would also destroy tanks during *Barbarossa*.

to find Budyonny's staff, but they didn't know where Budyonny was. Zhukov made the most of the situation by ensuring that his mother and sister, who lived nearby, were evacuated, before moving on to Maloyaroslavets. Spotting two cars parked next to the local Party office, he found Budyonny inside with a small group of officers poring over a map, trying to guess where his Reserve Front staff might be. After a brief exchange, Zhukov promptly went back to Moscow. His report to the Stavka and Stalin was blunt:

> The main danger comes from the fact that all the roads towards Moscow are open, and the weak protection brought by the Mozhaysk Line is no guarantee against the arrival of the enemy's armored forces at Moscow's gates. We must immediately assemble forces, from wherever possible, on the Mozhaysk Line.

This candid assessment pleased the Vozhd. Budyonny was relieved of his command. Zhukov was given responsibility of the Western Front, which was promptly combined with the Reserve Front with Konev as deputy, but Stalin made it clear that both their lives depended on their success over the Germans.

The Enemy at the Gates of Moscow

Supported by the Stavka, Zhukov started straight away. A new Reserve Front was put in place before in its turn being placed under Zhukov's command, who by the 12th, oversaw the whole defense of the capital. He confirmed the dispatch of all the Red Army units available,

The 5cm Pak 38—maneuverable, compact and with a good firing rate—was an adequate antitank piece, but found its limitations when it came into service in the summer of 1941, and had to face KVs and T-34s. The one in the photograph is said to have destroyed seven Soviet tanks. (Jacobsen/ECPAD/Defense)

A destroyed Soviet motorized column. The trucks seem to be GAZ-AA, nicknamed "Russki-Ford" by the Germans. (Heinrich Freytag/ECPAD/Defense)

the militia and the military schools in order to rebuild a front on the incomplete Mozhaysk Line. On the ground, resources already available had been deployed, either by order of Zhukov's staff, or by individuals showing initiative, as with Major G. Starchak, commander of the paratrooper school at Yukhnov. He assembled 400 men, including members of the NKVD, and blocked the attempt by the reconnaissance group of the 10th Panzer Division to take the Ugra bridge. The arrival of a heavily armed motorized battalion forced the Russians to fall back. Russian sources claimed that Starchak's men managed to destroy the bridge. The Stavka had already sent 3,500 cadets, from the infantry and artillery schools in Podolsk, east with orders to last at least four to five days. The situation implied resistance at all costs. Zhukov imposed a draconian discipline, including hunting down anyone too slow, deserters and other "trouble-makers," civilian or military, though this was not really anything new.

Even though he had found the ideal general to defend Moscow, Stalin, though hoping for the best, prepared for the worst. On the 9th, he ordered the closure of over a thousand businesses. The day after, all inhabitants who were not employed in the armament industry were requisitioned as laborers to build fortifications. This measure was not unusual since the summer and the Muscovites got on with it more or less willingly. However, they quickly realized the seriousness of the situation. Firstly, no fewer than 250,000 civilians, especially women, were mobilized to build a new line close to the city, to be finished within four weeks. But the danger was getting closer, first in the air. Olga Sapozhnika remembered: "We were taken several kilometers away from Moscow, we were a large number and we were asked to

These men from the 293rd Infantry Division are interrogating prisoners—possibly deserters. Summary executions abounded as early as the beginning of *Barbarossa*, in keeping with Nazi indoctrination and orders. The car is a SdKfz 2 Type 170 VK. (Otto Paul/ECPAD/Defense)

It is difficult to find shots of Soviet soldiers, especially at the beginning of *Typhoon*. This photograph clearly demonstrates the difficulties of transporting the wounded— who were often left behind. Several generals were wounded during *Typhoon*, among them Eremenko, commander of the Bryansk Front. (Ph. Rio Collection)

dig trenches. On the first day, we were shot at by a Fritz who dove on us. Eleven girls were killed and four wounded."

Other preparatory measures added to the concern felt by the population and the foreign chancelleries, resulting in what became known as "the Moscow Panic." Scenes of pillaging and panic took place everywhere as thousands of civilians were evacuated, but the authorities remained in control. On the 14th, Stalin ordered the departure of the main theaters, then the university, then foreign representatives. Coming out of a conference on the military situation on the 11th, the British ambassador wrote: "it was a hopeless report … Moscow's position is extremely precarious." The US military attaché's assessment was even more final: "the end of the Russian opposition is near."

The End of the Vyazma Pocket

The battles of the pockets started as soon as they were closed up, the Red Army troops trapped between the infantry and the panzers. The largest part of Army Group Center was concentrated to the east of Vyazma, encompassing most of the 16th, 19th, 20th and 32nd armies—the latter from the Reserve Front—which totaled at least 500,000 men—in a pocket initially 75km by 35km. The 24th Army of the Reserve Front had already shattered into several smaller pockets in the south. Its commander, General Rakutin, was killed on October 10, whilst trying to break through the encirclement.

The woodland terrain concealed movements but complicated the coordination between the troops who quickly ran out of ammunition, and more importantly food and medical supplies. The VVS provided a few airdrops, but it was not enough, especially as the pocket was reduced drastically in a few days under pressure from the infantry. As soon as they were spotted a deluge of shells and bombs rained down on the *frontoviki*. Whilst the fog on the 9th limited considerably the Luftwaffe's sorties (139), they totaled over 500 the next day. On the 10th, the pocket measured just 20km by 20km. Inside, the armies of the Western Front were now under command of General Ivan Boldin. Despite his failure against 3rd Panzer Group, Konev still trusted his subordinate, whom he ordered to break through; after all, Boldin escaped from the Minsk pocket in July. As for Zhukov, he needed more time, and therefore called for the surrounded troops to fight until their last breath, which many would do.

Boldin managed to break through on the 11th and 12th, south of Vyazma in the sector held by the XLVI Panzer Corps. Poorly coordinated, lacking support weapons and artillery, the Russians sent veritable human waves, supported as much as possible by the tanks available. Whilst they tried to attack mostly under the cover of darkness, the urgency of the situation sometimes forced them to charge in broad daylight. In the early hours of the 12th, some men even managed to reach the command post of Lieutenant General Hans-Karl von Eseback, commander of the 11th Panzer Division. The officer and his staff were taken aback but were saved at the last minute by the tanks they had kept in reserve, which pushed the riflemen back, with "huge losses." The 5th Panzer Division, barely arrived at the front, saw itself propelled into the horror of the war in the east. On October 12 and 13, two *schützen* companies counted 2,000 dead in front of their line. It was similar for the 2nd Panzer Division positioned further south. An antitank artilleryman, H. E. Braun, remembers a nighttime attack when the rockets illuminated, first hundreds, then thousands

This Sturmgeschütz from 226th StuG Battalion is supporting infantry during a sweep operation in the undergrowth. In the foreground a *frontovik* surrenders to a *landser*. (Mortag/ECPAD/Defense)

This photograph of an anonymous *landser* illustrates how much a wreck can contribute to the protection of an individual foxhole against shrapnel—and the rain! The vehicle is a T-20 Komsomolets, built before the war and common in 1941. The self-propelled ZIS-30 was based on it. Note the 7.5cm le.IG 18 infantry gun in the background. (Jacobsen/ECPAD/Defense)

of Soviet soldiers, with Cossack cavalrymen and columns of trucks advancing towards the thin German front line. Braun even recalls that: "the brave soldiers, and in some places even the antitank gunmen with their pieces were trampled by this human tide, pushed to find an exit towards the east by the certainty of death." Perhaps the guarantee of being treated humanely by the victors might have made them more willing to surrender. Braun carries on: "then came the turn of the logistic services and staff, the cooks fought knife in hand next to their mobile food kitchens, and drivers were fighting for their lives."

Again the panzers intervened, this time the 2nd Panzer Division, opening fire at close range, "hitting men from the Red Army who had broken through and even their own men." It was the same scene north of the pocket and overall, deprived of their best asset, their mobility, the panzer divisions suffered significant losses, especially amongst their exhausted artillery. The 7th Panzer Division alone lost 700 soldiers in a few days, including 105 from a *schützen* company of 140 men. The Russians had some KVs available in this sector.

Despite German efforts, a significant number of Russians managed to escape. Boldin, though wounded, was one of them. If going out in force and taking advantage of the relatively low numbers of the German mechanized infantry was to lead to success—though always at a cost—many relied on discretion, or even hid, sometimes becoming a partisan detachment (*Otriad*). Some deserters tried to follow, avoiding their own troops as much as the Germans. Others waited for the departure of the German troops. Some groups regaining their lines did

A formation of StG 1 returning from a mission. Robust and equipped with a strong fixed landing gear, the Ju 87 Stuka was one of the aircraft that suffered the least from the mud on the airfields. The mechanics however, would end up removing, sometimes systematically, the fairings on the wheels to avoid the accumulation of debris. (Speck/ECPAD/Defense)

not waste any time and seized the opportunity to inflict losses on the enemy. On October 13, the central radio of Hoepner's Fourth Panzer Army, supposed to be in a safe zone, was the target of a surprise attack. The Germans mourned the loss of 60 men and a lot of resources. On the same day, the regimental diary of the XLVI Panzer Corps deplored the fact that: "the clearing up of the pocket southwest of Vyazma is taking longer than anticipated. Small enemy groups constantly appear which, with energetic command, offer a fierce resistance." Some runaways were lucky—Rokossovsky fled Vyazma on foot with his staff. On the way he met an NKVD squadron, who guided the group. Together they avoided the German patrols and, exploiting the rainy weather that limited visibility, made contact with the 18th Division in Gzhatsk on the 9th. The losses of the Red Army near Vyazma will never be known for sure, but by the 15th, when the pocket was reduced, they were disastrous, and there are many descriptions of the carnage. Teenager Maria Denisova, who lived in a village nearby, remembers that: "There were so many corpses everywhere. We trod on them as if the ground was made of them. They were next to each other and on top of another. Some had no legs, or heads or other body parts were missing. We had to tread on them because there was nowhere else to place our feet. Everything was covered by them, the river and its banks." The 15-year-old had to watch as her father was shot by the Germans for being a partisan; and her mother was killed by a grenade thrown into a cave where they had taken refuge.

General der Flieger, Wolfram von Richthofen, cousin of the famous Red Baron and chief of the Fliegerkorps VIII, remembered similar scenes whilst flying over the region in his Fi 156 Storch: "There are horrible scenes of destruction in the places where the Red Army soldiers tried to break through. The Russians have suffered a true blood bath. Piles of corpses, abandoned equipment and guns in pieces, are scattered everywhere." Despite the worsening weather, his machines had contributed to this destruction—the Luftflotte 2 had flown 900 sorties on October 12 and 13.

Surrendering to the Germans

Ideology, racial stereotypes, the brutality of the fighting, thirst for revenge, or even simply the wish not to "burden" themselves with prisoners, all contributed to explain behavior like that described by Wolfgang H, a soldier in a panzer division who discovered a group of terrified and unarmed Russian soldiers behind some wreckage. He ordered them to put their hands up, but they crowded together and put their faces in their hands. As they hadn't immediately "surrendered," he and his comrades then shot them, noting "It was commonplace for us to do this... They were cowards—they didn't deserve any better anyway."[1] Those who did manage to surrender did not necessarily escape brutality. Often weak, starved and sometimes wounded, their long march in low temperatures was an ordeal. A German soldier remembers: "After the two battles of Vyazma-Bryansk, when the prisoners were brought to the rear, far beyond Smolensk. I often took that road—the ditches on the side of the road were filled with slaughtered Russians. The cars had driven over them, it was horrible."

Any civilians who tried to give them food were often shot too. Army Group Center's defective logistics does not alone explain the inhumane conditions. A guard wrote to his family on October 15 that his camp was completely full, holding 7,000 prisoners, some of them wounded, and that 2,000 more had just arrived. By the 23rd there were 11,000, and 20,000 two days later. Mortality rates rocketed and some prisoners resorted to cannibalism to survive. Furthermore, the military police (GFP) and the SS services (SD, Einsatzgruppen) "skimmed" the ranks, looking for commissars and Jewish soldiers, who were summarily executed. Lax surveillance by the guards did however offer opportunities to the more audacious. Abram Gordon was a volunteer in the 113th Division, Budyonny's Front; as a Jew, he knew he had nothing to lose. Captured during an attempted breakthrough, he managed to hide in a hay bale on the side of the road, and then rejoined the Russian lines to fight once more. As with all escapees, he was interrogated according to the NKVD's regulations who were obsessed with spies. His religion made matters even worse: "How could you, as a Jew, escape from the Germans?"[2]

1 D. Stahel, *op.cit*, p.150.
2 D. Stahel reported a slightly different version of A. Gordon's testimony, here taken from C. Merridale, *Ivan's War*, p121–122.

A column of prisoners passing vehicles of Hoepner's 4th Panzer Group. Note the "H" on the Opel Blitz mudguard. Many of the prisoners are wearing civilian garb, indicating that they belong to a militia division. (Spieth/ECPAD/Defense)

Bryansk: A Partial Failure for Guderian?

The situation in Bryansk was quite different from the Vyazma sector. Eremenko's Bryansk Front was scattered into two different pockets, in a much larger zone and faced less concentrated German troops. Whilst Weich's Second Army pushed as planned from the west and northwest, Guderian's "Second Panzer Army" did not fulfill its task so efficiently in the east. General Mikhail Petrov's 50th Army was surrounded north of Bryansk, with Heinrici's XLIII Army Corps to one side, and the 18th Panzer Division and 112nd Infantry Division to the east. The armored division received for this occasion a welcome reinforcement, the Infantry Regiment Grossdeutschland, an elite unit from the Heer. Further south, a second pocket held the 3rd and 13th armies around Trubchevsk. Guderian entrusted the task of closing up this pocket to just the 29th Motorized Division, whilst the XXXV Army Corps took charge of the other sectors. A swampy, wooded region, it seemed to match the abilities of the 1st Cavalry Division serving in the XXXV Army Corps. However, the Red Army would prove more belligerent than at Vyazma.

Taking advantage of the relative weakness of the elements Guderian had left to hold the pockets, the surrounded troops promptly tried to escape. On the 9th, a strong group under the direct orders of General Petrov broke the 18th Panzer Division's line, before Grossdeutschland could arrive. During the fight General Petrov was mortally wounded, one of the three Soviet generals to die during the Vyazma and Bryansk battles (this modest number can be explained by the presence of a large number of colonels in positions usually allocated to generals). The battle continued over several days, the critical moment coming

A column of panzers moving through a village. The last Panzer III carries a second *rommelkiste*, a storage box affixed to the back of the turret. (Heinrich Freytag/ECPAD/Defense)

Order of Battle: Army Group Center

Field Marshal von Bock (October 2, 1941)

THIRD PANZER ARMY (Colonel General Hoth until October 5, 1941 then Colonel General Reinhardt)

XLI Panzer Corps (Colonel General Model):
1st Panzer Division (111 panzers), 36th Motorized Division, 6th Infantry Division

LVI Panzer Corps (General Schaal):
6th Panzer Division (108 Panzer 35(t)s plus ? other models),* 7th Panzer Division (128 Panzer 38(t)s and 68 other models), 14th Motorized Division, 129th Infantry Division

VI Army Corps (General Förster):
26th and 110th Infantry Divisions

V Army Corps (General Roff):
5th, 35th and 106th Infantry Divisions
Reserve: 900th Lehr Brigade (mot.), with a Sturmgeschütz battery

SECOND PANZER ARMY (Colonel General Guderian)

XXIV Panzer Corps (General Baron Geyr von Schweppenburg):
3rd Panzer Division (?), 4th Panzer Division (110 tanks, September 26), 10th Motorized Division

XLVII Panzer Corps (General Lemelsen):
17th Panzer Division (52 panzers plus 76 to be repaired, September 10), 18th Panzer Division (93 panzers plus 114 to be repaired, September 9), 29th Motorized Division

XLVIII Panzer Corps (General Kempf):
9th Panzer Division (62 panzers), 16th and 25th Motorized Divisions

XXXV Army Corps (General Kaempfe):
1st Cavalry Division, 95th, 262nd, 293rd and 296th Infantry Divisions

XXXIV Army Corps (General Metz):
45th and 134th Infantry Divisions

FOURTH PANZER ARMY (Colonel General Hoepner)

XL Panzer Corps (General Stumme):
2nd Panzer Division (184 panzers, September 30), 10th Panzer Division (152 panzers), 258th Infantry Division

XLVI Panzer Corps (General Vietinghoff):
5th Panzer Division (186 panzers, September 30), 11th Panzer Division (93 panzers), 252nd Infantry Division

LVII Panzer Corps (General Kuntzen):
19th Panzer Division (?, 16 Panzer 38(t)s received on October 4), 20th Panzer Division (?, 30 Panzer 38(t)s received on October 4), 2nd SS-Panzer Division Das Reich (with a StuG battery), 3rd Motorized Division

XII Army Corps (General Schroth):
34th and 98th Infantry Divisions

NINTH ARMY (Colonel General Strauss)

VIII Army Corps (General Heitz):
8th, 28th and 87th Infantry Divisions

XXIII Army Corps (General Schubert):
102nd, 206th, 251st and 256th Infantry Divisions

XXVII Army Corps (General Wäger):
86th, 162nd and 255th Infantry Divisions
Reserves and panzers: 161st Infantry Division; 184th, 189th, 210th StuG Battalions

SECOND ARMY (Colonel General Baron von Weichs)

XIII Army Corps (General Felber):
17th and 260th Infantry Divisions

XLIII Army Corps (General of Infantry Heinrici):
52nd and 131st (elements) Infantry Divisions

LIII Army Corps (General Weisenberger):
31st, 56th and 167th Infantry Divisions
Reserves: 112nd Infantry Division

FOURTH ARMY (Field Marshal von Kluge)

VII Army Corps (General Fahrmbacher):
7th, 23rd, 197th and 267th Infantry Divisions

IX Army Corps (General Geyer):
137th, 183rd, 263rd and 292nd Infantry Divisions

XX Army Corps (General Materna):
15th, 78th and 268th Infantry Divisions

Panzers: 191st and 202nd StuG Battalions

LUFTFLOTTE 2 (Field Marshal Kesselring)

II Air Corps (General Loerner)
Fighters: II and III/JG3; JG 51; I/JG52.
Bombers: I and II/KG3; III/KG26; I/KG28; I and III/KG53; KG 100.
Attack: II/SKG-210 (Bf 110 Fighter-bomber); StG 77 (Stukas).

VIII Air Corps (General von Richthofen)
Fighters: II/JG52; III (S) LG 2.
Bombers: I and III/KG 2; III/KG 3.
Stukas: II and III/StG 1; I and III/StG 2.

Total: 549 operational aircraft

* Panzer figures are from September 28 unless otherwise stated.

on October 13 and 14, in the woods around Karachev. The Russians opened a breach about 2km wide, and counterattacked at daybreak on the 13th. The 2nd Company of Regiment Grossdeutschland found itself isolated. The 11th Company soon came to the rescue, but the *frontoviki* maintained a heavy, relentless fire, using not only mortars and antitank guns, but also heavy howitzers and 8.5cm antiaircraft guns. With the support of the panzers, the Germans tried to retake the village of Annino and its bridge, over which the Russians were escaping. Some surrendered readily, but many were prepared to carry on fighting. But while the German infantry lacked ammunition, artillery fire caused enormous losses for the Russians. On the evening of the 14th, the situation seemed under control, but the tension was such that an officer from the Grossdeutschland was killed and another wounded by overly nervous guards. The regiment lost a total of five company commanders that day, but took more than 3,000 prisoners, amongst which was the 50th Army's staff.

In the southern pocket, Eremenko also organized an exit towards the east, taking advantage of a vast numerical superiority to pit nearly 12 divisions against the 29th Motorized Division. The general was wounded on the 13th and was evacuated by plane towards Moscow. When a suspicious Stalin came to visit him in hospital, he could report that: "[…] the troops have attacked the enemy perimeter for eight days and have finally managed to break through."

Two Panzer IIIs, from the 11th Panzer Division, in a burning village. The one in the foreground carries the division's two insignias, the ghost and the circle crossed by a vertical line. (Heinrich Freytag/ECPAD/Defense)

The bad weather hit the Luftwaffe in equal measure. This reconnaissance Fw 189 had to be serviced outdoors. The car is a Horch 901. (Walther Luben/ECPAD/Defense)

The main assault took place between the 11th and the 13th. Despite having an additional rifle battalion, the fighting was "bitter" according to the 29th Motorized Division. Notwithstanding the lack of tanks, it obtained the support of 39th Panzer Regiment of the 17th Panzer Division, which managed to plug some breaches. However, the *frontoviki* also exploited some swampy areas that were poorly covered by the 1st Cavalry Division. The arrival of the 10th and 25th Motorized Divisions, and the 9th Panzer Division—the last two coming from the XXXVII Panzer Corps—put an end to mass breakthroughs. But the pocket would not be fully eliminated until October 20. In the meantime, on the 13th, Guderian urgently requested the help of the XXIV Panzer Corps to eliminate a large group threatening the Second Panzer Army's rear. A day later, the 3rd Panzer Division sent a *kampfgruppe* composed of three companies of tanks, infantry and Paks, plus an artillery battery, that found … nothing.

While dozens or hundreds of isolated Russian troops ended up in the hands of the Germans, many more were able to escape, though without most of their equipment and their heavy weaponry. Doctor Natalia Peshkova and her group reached the Russian lines by trusting to the sun and travelling directly east, paying no attention to units of either side.

In the Trubchevsk pocket, seven of the 12 divisions managed, at least in part, to escape. Nevertheless, the same horror seen in Vyazma and Bryansk was found here too. Ernst Guicking, of 52nd Infantry Division, XLIII Army Corps, while "clearing" the northern pocket, wrote to his wife that: "[…] We are tripping up over dead Russians. It is truly horrific … more corpses than can be counted. A lot of women amongst them. No battlefield could be worse than this one."

The numbers confirm this. The two pockets saw the total destruction of seven Soviet armies out of the 16 present at the beginning of the battle, as well as 64 of 95 rifle divisions and 11 of 15 tank brigades, plus 50 of the 62 artillery regiments not allocated to a specific division. Only the cavalry seemed to come out unscathed, either because it found itself on the outside of the pockets or because it could exploit the terrain to escape the encirclements. Eight of the nine cavalry divisions survived the battle, but in what state? On October 15, the 53rd Division of Dovator's Cavalry Group was limited to 1,100 men, 45 machine guns and five guns; his commander asked for 800 rifles for as many unarmed soldiers. It was the same for the infantry. The surviving 113th Division only had 2,000 soldiers left by the end of the fighting in Vyazma; General I. A. Presnyakov, commander of the division was made prisoner. Of the 1.25 million men deployed, nearly 100,000 escaped the encirclements: the 22nd and 269th armies as well as Dovator's Cavalry Group from the Western Front, the 33rd Army from the Reserve Front and part of the Ermakov Group from the Bryansk Front. A further 85,000 managed to escape the Vyazma Pocket and 25,000 from the Bryansk. That leaves over a million Russian soldiers killed, taken prisoner or missing in action. When, on October 14, Bock proclaimed the Vyazma battle over, Army Group Center claimed nearly 510,000 prisoners, but also the capture or destruction of 876 tanks, 2,891 guns, 465 antitank guns, 355 antiaircraft guns and 46 aircraft. The next day, the figures increased by 50,000 prisoners, 200 tanks, 844 guns, and dozens of antitank and antiaircraft pieces. Around 97 percent of the Russian tanks present on September 30 had been lost. On October 19, the Army Group Centre commander announced that the two battles constituted "the greatest feat of the campaign," and the total number of prisoners, taking into account the various pockets, now reached, with Germanic precision, 673,098. At least seven generals

View of the back of a Panzer III, loaded with storage boxes, one of them bearing the ghost insignia. (Heinrich Freytag/ECPAD/Defense)

I had a comrade ... Two *landsers*, apparently from a panzer unit, pay their respects to their fallen comrade. As victorious as the Ostheer was, it also wore itself out in the battles of *Barbarossa*. (Heinrich Freytag/ECPAD/ Defense)

had been captured, including three army commanders: Philip Ershakov (20th Army), Mikhail Lukin (19th Army) and Sergei V. Vishnevsky (32nd Army). It could therefore be deduced that the Red Army lost more than 300,000 killed or missing in the carnage. The figures were even higher than the terrible outcome of the battle of Kiev. Paradoxically, this raised doubts in some German soldiers, like Hans von Luck, of the 7th Panzer Division: "After clearing up the Vyazma pocket, we have been wondering how Stalin could keep producing new divisions… And where these thousands of guns and tanks could be coming from?"

The German losses were obviously nothing close to these numbers. On October 15, Army Group Center was missing 48,000 men compared to the beginning of the month. They had inflicted 20 losses for one incurred. They were however, adding to those incurred since June, of which less than half had been replaced. The deterioration of the Ostheer continued. Furthermore, the situation in some units became critical. This was the case of the *schützen* regiment, 18th Panzer Division, or the 7th and 20th Panzer Divisions. The manpower crisis also worsened in the traditional infantry. The V Army Corps, attached to the Third Panzer Army, lost 3,500 men in *Typhoon*, and the IX Army Corps lost 5,000 during a victorious week of engagements near Yelnya. The arrival of the cold weather also worsened the state of the equipment. The 6th Panzer Division had only one mechanized section left after the damage sustained during the Boldin counterattacks. The 20th Panzer Division, though benefiting from robust and dependable Panzer 38(t)s and little involved during the offensive, only had 39 operational tanks by October 11. Finally, if the Timoshenko Army Group had just been annihilated, the "Judeo-Bolshevik threat" remained. Had the "decisive battle" announced by Hitler in his speech to the troops on October 1, before *Typhoon*, really been that decisive?

Strategy, Mud, and Logistics

At the end of the first week of Operation *Typhoon*, a German victory seemed to be on the horizon. The adversaries now had to devise their strategy for the rest of the campaign. The answer was quite simple on the Soviet side, but the German commanders abandoned all caution, even though other external factors were to have a large influence on events.

If the Kremlin and the Allied camp were worried, the Axis was gloating. Whilst the extent of the damage of the Vyazma-Bryansk battles would not be fully known until the end of October, the first reports seemed promising. From the 9th, German reports mentioned the encirclements. On the same day Dr Otto Dietrich, head of the Reich's press service, announced to a crowd of journalists that: "the campaign in the east has been victorious, thanks to the destruction of Timoshenko's Army Group." At this, journalists from Germany as well as their allied countries, stood up, gave the Nazi salute and shouted "Heil!" The next day, the headline of the Romanian daily newspaper, *Universul*, read: "The destruction of the Timoshenko Army Group means the end of the campaign in Russia," which probably did little to convince the soldiers of the Romanian Third Army who had been engaged in the bloody siege of Odessa for two months.

Even Soviet vehicles got stuck in the mud. Here, an SdKfz half-track tractor tows a Russki-Ford, recently captured, given its crude markings. The terrain, more than winter itself, damaged the machinery, the cold then striking the final blow. (Otto Paul/ECPAD/Defense)

Rain transformed earth runways into swamps. The Bf 109s, which had fragile landing gear, suffered badly. Once in the air though, with experienced pilots at their controls, using tried and tested tactics, the Bf 109 remained a plague for the Soviet air force, which was still recovering from the initial shock of *Barbarossa*. (Jacobsen/ECPAD/Defense)

Franco sent a telegram congratulating Hitler on his "final victory." The Nazi authorities were convinced. In occupied Poland, fireworks were stockpiled to celebrate the entry in Moscow. Hitler ordered a demolition team to prepare to blow up the Kremlin. Berlin's cinemas announced the upcoming screening of a documentary entitled "The Germans enter Moscow." However many others remained cautious. Goebbels, in charge of propaganda, deplored the fact that the press was "too optimistic and positive." Mussolini had doubts, as did Ciano, his Foreign Affairs minister and son-in-law, who wrote in his diary: "[…] will we not read simply that the front has been pushed one or two hundred kilometers further?" In fact, the tone of the press changed quickly. On October 11, the *Universul* headline read, "The collapse is near." At the rear, just as at the front, such babel was treated with skepticism. General Gunther Blumentritt, of the OKH, felt that "the troops […] do not appreciate the propaganda's exaggerations any longer," even if most still had faith in Hitler. But the Führer and his most senior generals appeared to fall victim to this wave of optimism and adopted a ludicrous strategy.

"Deutschland Siegt an Allen Fronten"[1]

Now the initial phase of *Typhoon* had been completed, came the matter of how to proceed. Several weeks after the Kiev disaster—in which the Red Army lost more than 616,000 men, killed, made prisoner, or missing—the destruction of Timoshenko's Army Group

---

1   Germany is victorious on all fronts.

This Sturmgeschütz, 177th StuG Battalion (the griffon insignia is just visible), has slid into a pool of mud, taking with it a long bridge, in conditions that illustrate the *rasputitsa* perfectly. This group of assault guns initially operated in Guderian's panzer group's northern zone of engagement, whose vehicle can be seen.

convinced Hitler and the OKH that the enemy was on his knees. On October 7, the Führer visited Bock's HQ to study the second phase. *Typhoon* continued with divergent efforts north and south of the capital, in order to destroy the last remnants of the Red Army at the center of the Western Front. In the north, the Third Panzer Army, followed by the Ninth Army, pursued the remains of the Western Front towards Rzhev and Kalinin. In the south, the Second Panzer Army had to send the XXIV Panzer Corps alone towards Tula; Kempf's XLVIII Panzer Corps, until now little engaged, went west towards Kursk before rejoining the XXIV Panzer Corps. Only the Fourth Panzer Army and the Fourth Army marched on towards Moscow from the west. Hoepner initially had to leave—like Guderian—the necessary troops to deal with the various Soviet pockets. A genuine arrogance, based upon contempt of an often-underestimated opponent, prevailed. Why worry about an already beaten enemy? Thus, the Oberkommando der Luftwaffe (OKL) told the Luftflotte 2 units that they could be redeployed elsewhere. And Richthofen learned that his Fliegerkorps VIII would spend New Year's Eve in Germany. The plan was confirmed when, on the 13th, Hitler ordered the capital surrounded. He insisted however that the besiegers should not advance past the railway track that encompassed the city. Just as at Leningrad, as part of his *Vernichtungskrieg* (war of extermination) the Führer was forbidding any street fighting,

These two photographs show endless columns of prisoners passing German vehicles, including a Renault AGR truck. Note the rather lax surveillance, which the most determined took advantage of to escape. (Speck/ECPAD/Defense)

Whilst the *frontoviki* move towards prison camps where many will meet their deaths, the *landsers* continue marching east. The first snow has fallen, but the temperatures and the condition of the roads are not problematic. (Speck/ECPAD/Defense)

preferring a war of attrition, starving its defenders and the population. The Kremlin's destruction would have to wait a little.

How was the new strategy received in Army Group Center? The disagreements continued. The reduction of the pockets proved easier than the German generals had originally anticipated, thanks to the good weather and the fact that the Soviets did not attack from the east. The surrounded soldiers were therefore left to their own devices, although it was still necessary to devote the means to reduce the pockets. Guderian had not done this for the Bryansk pocket, to Bock's great annoyance. Bock reproached him—with good reason—as he had made the same mistake at the end of July in Smolensk. So far the *blitzkrieg* of *Schnelle Heinz* ("Fast Heinz"), victim of the weather and moreover poor logistics, had not impressed.

Of course, the very same factors had affected the other armies, and several generals immediately started to criticize. Hoepner deplored the fact that: "[it] seems once again that we are given objectives, which in view of our resources, are too far-reached; we are aiming for too many objectives at once." He requested, in vain, that rather than advancing towards Kalinin like "a lost child," the Third Panzer Army should assault towards Moscow. Furthermore, whilst launching Army Group Center in this vast maneuver around the capital, Hitler had left Army Groups North and South to pursue their own offensives. On October 16, two army corps launched an offensive towards Tikhvin to strengthen the Leningrad blockade. Added to this were disagreements over doctrine. Kluge spent a lot of time dealing with the Vyazma pocket and Hoepner had to wait a long time for his infantry divisions to

The initial successes of *Typhoon* led to the hasty construction of fortifications in Moscow itself. These civilians are wearing warm clothing because the temperatures are starting to drop. However, the majority of the workers consisted of women and elderly people. The needs of the front and the industry had already taken its toll on the male population. (RIA Novosti)

Colonel General Baron Maximilian von Weichs, commander of the Second Army, walking out of the headquarters of his LIII Army Corps, which was moved to Bryansk, allowing us to date this photograph to mid-October at the earliest. Weichs was one of the rare generals to retain Hitler's respect throughout the conflict. (Koll/ECPAD/ Defense)

The rigors of the Russian fall weather are clearly already being felt by these panzerjäger troops. The Pak 38 only comprised 8 percent of the Ostheer's antitank guns in June 1941. (Heinrich Freytag/ECPAD/Defense)

arrive when his panzers came up against fortified lines that they struggled to overcome on their own. Finally, on the ground German generals made several mistakes on an operational and tactical level, which allowed the Soviets to gain some time.

The pursuit that started on October 8 was also disrupted by another factor, which in itself was not exactly surprising.

It Snowed…

From October 6, the weather changed. Near Bryansk that day the temperatures dropped and the wind rose. In the evening rain came, then snow. Early the next morning, the first rays of sunshine fell on fields and roads transformed into vast expanses of mud. The effect was immediate. That day, the 3rd Panzer Division's trucks remained stuck between Kromy and Orel. The Grossdeutschland, reinforcing the 18th Panzer Division, suffered a lot of mechanical problems. And if several generals had been waiting for—and fearing—this moment, it seemed to take some troops by surprise. Max Kuhnert of the 1st Cavalry Division stated:

> Suddenly, our task in Russia seemed insurmountable, our supplies were stuck, just like our heavy artillery, even with draught horses. The tanks laboriously made their way through the mud, which hindered their progress and used up more fuel than anticipated. We had the impression that the whole of Russia has turned into an enormous puddle of sticky mud and that we were stuck in the middle.

It is true that the Russian call this time of year the *rasputitsa*, the season without roads. The situation turned into a nightmare for Army Group Center, especially between October 9 and 11, when it was particularly rainy. The vehicles' fuel consumption shot up, as did breakdowns, and more than a few vehicles had to be abandoned due to lack of means of traction. Moreover, the drop in the nighttime temperatures, now often below zero, prevented the machines' recovery, as they were literally frozen to the ground. Even the panzers' tracks proved too narrow to make their way in these conditions. Already victims of the tough local conditions, the conditions of the horses worsened, but they remained indispensable to pull the artillery and the infantry's supply carts. In the 52nd Infantry Division, Second Army, they doubled the horse teams, but even this only enabled two of the four light battery pieces to be moved. The heavy battery pieces could not be moved at all.

What was the true impact of the mud during *Typhoon*? The snow fell mostly around Bryansk between October 7 and 13. The Rzhev region, further north, was spared. And everywhere, the German advance continued, sometimes quite quickly, like near Kalinin, exploiting each thaw and increase in temperature. What's more the *rasputitsa* disrupted the Red Army just as much, though they were on the defensive and slightly better prepared. Later German generals would largely exploit the weather—and Hitler's mistakes—to explain their

This 226th StuG Battalion sidecar is managing a muddy Russian track rather well. The Russian campaign spelled the end of motorcyclist battalions in the Ostheer, victims of their equipment's wear and tear and their losses not being compensated. Nevertheless, motorbikes and sidecars were still widely used as liaison vehicles. (Larz Heinz Müller/ECPAD/Defense)

In Profile:
German Vehicles

Panzerfunkwagen (Sdfz
263) 8-Rad, 7th Panzer
Reconnaissance Battalion,
4th Panzer Division, Orel,
October 4, 1941.

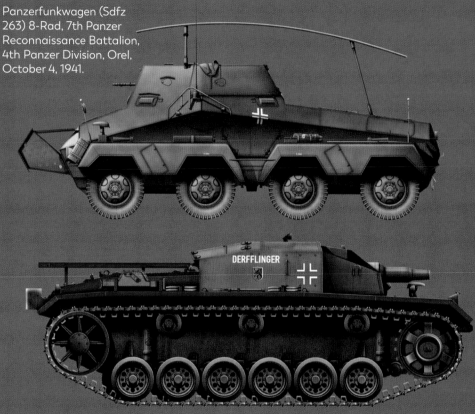

Sturmgeschütz III Ausf. C, 177th Sturmgeschütz
Battalion (then attached to the XIII Army Corps,
Second Army), Roslav, October 2, 1941.

Henschel Type 33
Einheitsdiesel, Fourth Army,
Yelnya, October 13, 1941.

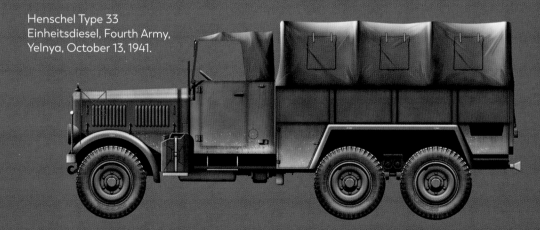

failures. But the *rasputitsa* arrived late that year, allowing the rapid initial advances. Goebbels was somehow right to rejoice in the weather at the beginning of *Typhoon*. The generals came to wish for the cold weather's arrival, like Hoepner who wished for "a fortnight of frost" to surround Moscow. Yet, as will be seen, another factor would play an even more crucial role.

Nevertheless, the effect of the mud and the cold on the equipment and the morale of both sides, must not be underestimated. On the 7th, Grossman rejoiced that: "there is rain, snow, hailstones, a bottomless, liquid swamp—a black paste, stirred by thousands of boots, wheels, tracks. And everyone is happy again. The Germans must be bogged down in our terrible fall." A German soldier for his part reported that: "each one of us thought of the same thing when he looked at the snowflakes falling on the muddy roads. The first sign of winter! How cold can the winter be and how long can it last?"

Bock worried especially, and with good reason, about the weather forecast and its effect on the morale and physical condition of the troops, already tired from such a long campaign. And winter supplies were still lacking.

Yes, winter was coming.

The Failure of Logistics

In reality, German misfortunes had roots in deficiencies that pre-dated *Typhoon*. There were supply issues even before the arrival of the fall rains, especially in Guderian's army. There had been a fuel shortage four days before the beginning of the *rasputitsa*. The famous Kampfgruppe Eberbach had to leave behind units in its wake, all the way to Orel. The taking of this town owed more to the initial surprise and the slowness of the enemy's reaction. But launching an offensive with only half the necessary fuel could only lead to significant problems, and the 4th Panzer Division was no exception to the rule. On the 4th, its vanguard was 200km away from the nearest fuel depot, and its trucks could only transport half the fuel necessary for Kampfgruppe Eberbach to travel 100km, once the quantity they themselves needed was deducted. It therefore took two days to resupply the whole of the *kampfgruppe*. Guderian asked the Luftwaffe for help, especially as he controlled Orel's southern aerodrome. But the Luftwaffe refused to risk its precious Ju 52s as Soviet fighters often appeared in those sectors that the Bf 109s could not cover. The hardware also suffered on the charge to Orel. On October 3, the 35th Panzer Regiment only had 59 operational machines, from 100 on September 30—only six Panzer IIIs and IVs had been lost in actual battle. In short, the 4th Panzer Division spent two days almost immobilized, due to lack of fuel, well before the rains came. Then, in order to leave for Mtsensk, Eberbach literally ransacked the 3rd Panzer Division's supplies, condemning them to a static role for the next few days. The same thing happened to the XLVIII Panzer Corps that finally arrived in the sector, but had to tighten its belt to help Kampfgruppe Eberbach. When, on the 6th, the main force of the XXIV Panzer Corps left for Mtsensk, it advanced quite alone.

This situation was not unique. The advance towards Kalinin having been deemed less crucial, Reinhardt's and Strauss's armies would have to make do with the meager share of an increasingly difficult resupply, because of their growing distance from the logistics

Weichs's motorcyclist escorts ready to lead the general's superb Maybach Zeppelin. The car bears both the "W" and the stag head of the Second Army. (Koll/ECPAD/Defense)

bases. They only received four trains of fuel between October 23 and November 13, fuel they of course had to move with worn-out trucks on muddy roads. Even Hoepner was not spared, with 50 percent of his trucks out of action when *Typhoon* started. The Fourth Army complained about the lack of fuel from October 8, whilst the Second Army asked for three times more supply trains. The supply situation then further worsened with the coming of winter. In September 2,093 trains had arrived across the whole front, but in October there were only 1,860 and their numbers continued to decrease. More than air raids and the odd partisan attack, the railway network was suffering from equipment problems—the German engines were not designed to operate in the cold climate and there was a shortage of rolling stock appropriate for use on the Russian network. Often the truck convoys waited in vain for a pre-arranged train until eventually, desperate for supplies, the troops helped themselves from the cargo destined for other units. With the demands for fuel and ammunition, winter equipment dropped to the bottom of the list. The merciless pillaging at the expanse of the population resolved the food problem, but the winter of 1812 was on the invaders' minds. General Wagner noted that "the campaign takes the risky look of a race against winter." But once more the German commanders preferred to follow the Nazi precepts rather than strategic common sense. "One has to take the most extreme risks in matters of logistics, for the greater good of the operational notion," declared Halder.

Mtsensk, Maloyaroslavets, and Mozhaysk

Although the battles of Vyazma and Bryansk were crushing victories for the Ostheer, the Red Army maintained its fighting spirit. In the days following, three engagements testified that the war in the east was not coming to an end, as the German high command had hoped.

Dmitry Lelyushenko, commander of the 1st Guards Rifle Corps had the ideal profile to oppose von Schweppenburg's XXIV Panzer Corps, which had just seized Orel. Just like Zhukov, he would prove to be the man for the job. He immediately showed the initiative and energy indispensable in times of crisis. Arriving at the Artillery School in Tula, he

It wasn't just the Ostheer cobbling together self-propelled antitank guns. The ZIS-30 was a combination of the powerful 57mm antitank gun, the ZIS-2, on a Komsomolets armored tractor. The result was a vulnerable machine carrying only 25 shells, but nevertheless proved quite mobile. In theory a battery of eight pieces served in each brigade engaged around Moscow. A hundred were built in Gorki.

Panzerzug n. 28 was one of ten armored trains committed during *Barbarossa*. Assigned to Army Group Center, it patrolled the Bryansk and Orel regions after *Typhoon*. Cobbled together in 1942, it comprised a captured engine and some captured armored wagons. Note the Somua S-35, one of the three it was supposed to carry, which allowed it to intervene away from the tracks. (Bundesarchiv 1011-139-1103-19)

In Profile:
Dmitry Lelyushenko

Born in 1901, Dmitry Lelyushenko was, like Zhukov, a veteran of the Great War and the Civil War. Infantryman, then cavalryman, he attended the Frunze Military Academy, and joined the Armored Army in the early 1930s. He was made a Hero of the Soviet Union for personal bravery while in command of a tank brigade during the Winter War in Finland—he would receive a second award for his actions near Maleshov in 1945. He was promoted to major general in the spring of 1941 and given command of the 21st Mechanized Corps. On June 28, at Daugavpils, he led his corps in a counterattack on the LVI Panzer Corps led by a certain Erich von Manstein, blocking it for a time. In August Stalin tasked him with forming 22 tank brigades in the region of Moscow. He spent a year defending Moscow before taking command of 1st Guards Army. His subsequent battlefield commands were successful and he ended the war directing forces during the Red Army's offensives against Berlin and Prague.

The first frosts gave hope to Army Group Center, bogged down in front of Moscow. This convoy could even use trailers to transport extra supplies. The one on the last truck resembles the horse-drawn, metal Stahlfeldwagen Hf. 7, nicknamed *Pferdemörder* (horse killer) due to its weight. (Jacobsen/ECPAD/Defense)

mobilized the staff, then because of the lack of appropriate vehicles, ordered the requisition of the town's buses to tow the guns. In addition to the 34th NVKD Regiment, Lelyushenko positioned the 36th Motorcyclist Regiment, a few militia units, some elements of the 5th Airborne Corps, and of course the tanks of Colonel Mikhail Katukov's 4th Tank Brigade. The paratroopers of the 201st Brigade fighting in the northern suburbs of Orel, received the support of two tank companies from the 4th—19 T-34s and two KVs—that Katukov sent on a "forceful reconnaissance." Bitter fighting erupted around the train station when the Germans tried to advance into the town from the north. The Germans deployed two 8.8cm Flaks and at the cost of just one Panzer IV, destroyed four enemy tanks, including the two KVs. Lelyushenko however, exploited the respite offered by the logistical problems suffered by General von Langermann's division. He deployed the NKVD Regiment, Katukov's two companies and the paratroopers escaped from Orel, 10km north on the road leading to Mtsensk. The aircraft of 5th Airborne Corps continued to make supply trips until the 6th, bringing reinforcements and ammunition. And whilst some promised reinforcements did not arrive, he did receive two batteries of Katyusha multiple rocket launchers. While Lelyushenko's forces were slowly being built up in Orel, by October 5, Langermann could only send one *vorausabteilung* (vanguard) centered around his motorcyclist battalion. Stalled at a roadblock built on Lelyushenko's instructions, and despite the support offered by some late-arriving panzers, he had to retreat. On this occasion the Russians captured a wounded soldier who helped identify the German panzer division. This information led Lelyushenko and Katukov to fall back with their tanks and prepare accordingly. When the panzer divisions advanced again, on the 6th, the defenders were prepared.

The Heroes of Mtsensk

The *kampfgruppe* marching on Mtsensk then Tula on October 6 was even weaker than Kampfgruppe Eberbach on September 30. It was, once again, just a vanguard that Colonel Eberbach entrusted to his deputy in charge of 35th Panzer Regiment, Major Meinrad von Lauchert. In fact, due to the lack of fuel, several units had remained in Orel. Nevertheless, the Germans, scalded by the skirmish the day before, made sure to take their 8.8cm and 10.5cm pieces, which up until now had always been able to neutralize the T-34s and the KVs. But where was this enemy? Lauchert went beyond the site of the previous day's ambush without meeting any resistance and approached his first objective, the bridge on the Lisitsa river. It was intact. Was this another blunder by the Russians? Not this time. To give Lelyushenko the time he needed, Katukov had planned a trap. He had sacrificed an NKVD detachment, well armed with 45mm antitank guns and four BT-7s, positioned at the end of the bridge. The colonel then concealed most of his tanks 400m away, on the crest of a hill. At 10:00, Lauchert had his artillery open fire before launching his tanks, eliminating easily "the defenders."

It was 11:30 when the major sent two panzer companies, followed by motorcyclists, toward

Vorausabteilung von Lauchert (October 6, 1941)

Staff, 35th Panzer Regiment (Major Meinrad von Lauchert)

Tanks

1st Battalion, 35th Panzer Regiment

5th Panzer Regiment (Medium Tanks Company, Panzer II and III)

Infantry

34th Motorcycle Battalion (cf. Kampfgruppe Eberbach, p.31)

3rd Company, 7th Reconnaissance Battalion (Reconnaissance Group Support Company)

Artillery

2nd Battalion, 103rd Artillery Regiment (cf. Kampfgruppe Eberbach, minus a battery)

1st Battalion, 53rd Nebelwerfer Regiment (cf. Kampfgruppe Eberbach)

2nd Battery, 60th Artillery Regiment (cf. Kampfgruppe Eberbach)

AntiAircraft Defense

2nd Battalion, 11th Anti-Aircraft Regiment (Heavy battery, 8.8cm and 2cm pieces)

Operation *Typhoon*: September 30–October 15, 1941

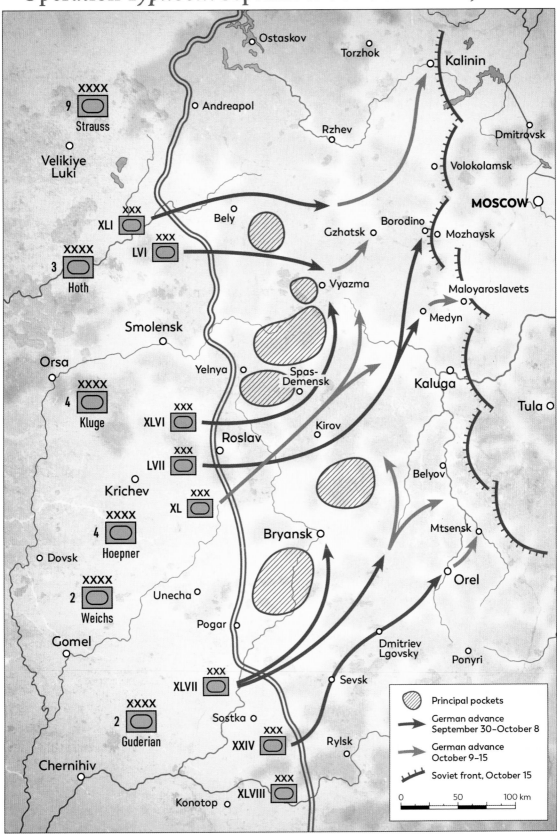

Legend:

- Principal pockets
- German advance September 30–October 8
- German advance October 9–15
- Soviet front, October 15

0   50   100 km

Soviet Tank Brigades—Born of Exigency

At the end of July 1941, the Stavka dissolved the last great mechanized units of the Red Army. The mechanized corps and independent tank divisions had proved their inefficiencies, suffering defeat after defeat. Due to a lack of competent staff and equipment—like radios—the Red Army simply could not master the war that the Ostheer imposed upon them. Tanks remained essential though and Lieutenant General Yakov Fedorenko, Chief Inspector of armored troops, convinced the Stavka to organize tanks in brigades.

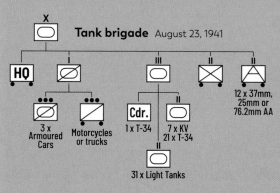

These units offered a number of advantages in that they could be created quickly, their format and size matched the competence of available officers, they could be positioned along the entire front, and the infantry and sometimes artillery in the brigade offered support to the tanks. Towards the end of August, nine brigades were formed between Leningrad, Moscow, and Kharkov. A month later 57 existed or were being formed.

The first brigades corresponded to Fedorenko's wishes and some even benefited from significant support, such as the 12th created in Kharkov with two small artillery and anti-aircraft battalions. The 4th Brigade formed in Stalingrad and placed under command of Colonel Mikhail Katukov received 30 light BT-7s and above all, 30 brand-new T-34s. Unfortunately the disrupted tank production could not always satisfy demand. Furthermore, combat quickly used up the brigades, which were sometimes extirpated in a matter of days, six being destroyed in October. From mid-September, a more austere organization was needed, with the disappearance of a battalion of tanks and of the artillery. As the fall battles played out, it was almost impossible to find two identical brigades. Some only possessed old worn-out models; the organizational table at right, from September, often bore little similarity to the reality on the ground. British support was still only virtual: the first 20 Valentines arrived in Archangel on October 11.

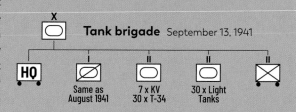

At the end of September, in the face of the Ostheer's 19 panzer divisions, the Red Army was able to field 30 tank brigades, a myriad of battalions with at most 30 machines and a handful of tank divisions, the latter being disbanded or converted to motorized formations, like the 101st Division of the Western Front. Nevertheless, an increasing number of brigades saw the light of day, 75 before the end of the year. And despite their weaknesses, they played a decisive role during *Typhoon*.

The T-40, an amphibious vehicle, was intended for reconnaissance, but necessity ruled and it was integrated into tank brigades. Armed only with machine guns and with thin armor, it was highly vulnerable. This column is unloading from a train.

the crest. Being careful, he also deployed a battery of 10.5cm and 8.8cm guns. The Russians seemed to have disappeared. In fact T-34s and KVs, camouflaged in the thickets on both sides of the road, were waiting for the first Panzer III to reach the top of the slope to open fire. The precision of the shots was somewhat off because only one of them was destroyed and the others returned fire. The Germans quickly realized they were outnumbered and outgunned and the panzers fell back in a cloud of smoke whilst their artillerymen hastily set up their batteries, and the motorcyclists ran for cover. But it was ten minutes before the heavy guns were brought to bear. One 8.8cm was able to hit Sergeant Ivan T. Lyubushkin's T-34, wounding the four crew, before it was destroyed by the nearest tank. The second 8.8cm fired three times before meeting the same fate. The huge 10.5cm K18 managed to destroy a T-34 before it was neutralized in its turn. This was too much for Lauchert, who ordered a retreat.

The motorcyclists jumped on their machines while the tanks backed away, masking their movements with smoke grenades, but still firing. Captain Vadimir Gusev then launched a battalion—composed of 21 T-34s and four KVs—forward. It was the first time that the 4th Panzer Division had faced this many heavy tanks. Lyubushkin's T-34, having recovered in the meantime, claimed no fewer than five panzers. But the 103rd Artillery Regiment battery remained—firing, covering its comrades. The 10.5cm howitzers destroyed three T-34s but the others kept on moving forward, crushing two pieces and several vehicles. A KV was immobilized and a few audacious artillerymen jumped on the powerless giant with fuel cans and set fire to it. As the Germans backtracked all the way to the west bank of the Lisitsa, Katukov ordered his tanks to return to their initial position. That night saw the first snow fall.

This rather small skirmish—each deploying roughly a large tank battalion and some support units—had a major impact on several levels, though the losses were rather modest and the Russian losses were worse. Katukov's forces saw a KV-1, two T-34s and four BT-7s completely destroyed, 300 men killed or taken prisoners and 11 antitank guns lost. The *Vorausabteilung* lost ten tanks—six of which were completely destroyed—five artillery pieces and ten dead.[1]

1   The German numbers are taken from J. Neumann, op. cit., p.314. But his numbers concerning the Soviet tanks are fanciful: 17 tanks destroyed out of 45 engaged.

A line of T-34s loaded with infantrymen moves up to the front, perhaps elements of one of the tank brigades deployed on the road to Moscow. The mass deployment of T-34s from October 1941 marked a new phase in the use of this excellent tank. Unfortunately, the lack of support and means of repair often counter-balanced this mass effect.

The Superiority of the T-34

The German defeat lay in the tactics and techniques. Firstly, for the first time the Red Army had used its most powerful tanks efficiently, and by using them *en masse*, had made a decisive impact in the engagement. Katukov and Lelyushenko would make sure that this lesson would never be forgotten. Secondly, this demonstration of the T-34's superiority over the Panzer III finally made Guderian and more generally the German commanders, take note of the Russian tank's characteristics—slanted armor, large tracks, long gun—and considered developing a machine capable of fighting it. (The German answer to the T-34 would be the famous Panzer V Panther.) Finally the 4th Panzer Division, even before the *rasputitsa*, was clearly defeated. Guderian's *kampfgruppe* could not win a frontal assault against Katukov's brigade. The colonel had gained the time Lelyushenko needed.

Whilst Eberbach was not the kind of officer to give up easily, the 4th Panzer Division had just been stopped in its tracks. Already poorly supplied, it was now unable to make vast maneuvers on such a muddy terrain. But Katukov's situation was not enviable. Lelyushenko was keeping the 11th Tank Brigade—50 machines, including several T-34s and KVs—in reserve, however he gave Katukov two multiple rocket launcher batteries, though these did not make up for his lack of troops. But Lelyushenko still needed more time to build up a line of resistance north of Mtsensk. Thankfully, Katukov's tanks lent themselves well to a mobile defense. When the 12th Schützen Regiment crossed the river from the east and began a flanking movement, Katukov slowly backed away towards the north. Eberbach and Lauchert were hard-pressed to give chase, given their own logistics issues. By then they only had 30 armor-piercing shells left for the three remaining 10.5cm K18s. The careful advance continued the day after, the riflemen marched towards the front line, leaving behind their bogged-down trucks. The 3rd Panzer Division remained unable to support its neighbor, apart from a modest *kampfgruppe* on its left flank. Nevertheless, on the 9th, Eberbach thought they would be able to reach Mtsensk, now less than 10 km away, with their fuel tanks and ammunition racks almost full. This time the "motorized" infantry maneuvered, still on foot, around the flanks to overtake Katukov's tanks, whilst Lauchert's panzers carefully progressed along the road, with artillery, antitank guns and the Luftwaffe—a group of Bf 109s was now based in Orel—ready to intervene. Despite these precautions, Katukov again, came out of this engagement victorious. The T-34s proved to be too dangerous a prey for the German infantry and set alight several panzers. The Soviet Air Force in their turn came to harass the 4th Panzer Division. The Germans only gained a few kilometers west of Mtsensk, whilst the 35th Panzer Regiment saw its number of operational tanks drop to thirty.

The crew of this 45mm antitank gun engage the enemy. They are wearing the padded jacket M1938, standard wear for the Red Army during the cold season. The gun was efficient against most panzers; but the front armor on the latest models of Panzer III, IV and the StuG resisted its impact well.

A Panzer IV overtakes an infantry column during the first snowfall. The cold was not as yet overly harsh, even though the temperatures had clearly dropped. As shown in this photograph, the mud slowed the Ostheer down more than the ice. (Bundesarchiv 101I73-2810-20a)

Repeating the Success of Orel

To make matters worse, further snowfall worsened the state of the roads, as well as drastically reducing visibility. Some German scouts discovered an undamaged pontoon on the Zusha river, southeast of Mtsensk. Eberbach was not the kind of man to let this opportunity pass him by. He sent First Lieutenant A. Wollschlager's panzers with a *schützen* company to take Mtsensk by the south, probably hoping for a repetition of his success in Orel a week earlier. The operation was a success … until the pontoon collapsed before the supporting 8.8cm pieces could get across. The small numbers of Russian infantrymen—and a certain lack of vigilance—were paid for dearly when the panzers enter Mtsensk around 12:00 on October 11. The panzers swept aside any opposition, some of the supporting infantry and settled in the north of the town, isolating Katukov's tanks west of the river. Lelyushenko tried to come to the aid of Katukov, who was trying to force a corridor with a tank company. But without infantry, the T-34s were vulnerable in front of the Panzer IIIs and the *schützen* roaming the town. Only three of the eight tanks were destroyed, their armor still resistant to the 5cm Panzergranate, with the survivors simply escaping towards the east. Wollschlager's situation took a turn for the worse though, when six KV-1s of the 11th Brigade, sent by Lelyushenko, arrived. The pioneers of the 4th Panzer Division had managed to fix the pontoon in the meantime, and a 10.5cm K18 gun as well as antitank mines were waiting for the heavy Soviet tanks. Three were immobilized.

Eberbach sent infantry and artillery reinforcements at around 15:00. This time, an 88 destroyed three T-34s from nearly a thousand meters away. Katukov understood that he

On October 11, the arrival of Eberbach's panzers in Mtsensk allowed them to take their revenge after their failure on the 6th. These are vehicles from the 4th Brigade, including in the foreground a GAZ-AA truck and a T-34 1941 model.

A similar scene, perhaps even in the same place, here on Mira Street, where a ZIS-6 of the 9th Mortar Regiment of the Guard has been almost completely destroyed, beside another T-34. Note the 132mm BM-13 rockets, the principal model used during the Great Patriotic War.

Another scene of desolation in Mtsensk. This T-34 is said to be part of a group of four machines from the 11th Brigade sent to destroy the BM-13—BM being short for combat vehicle in Russian—so that secret weapons did not fall into the Germans' hands. Officer Vlasnko and his crew are said to have succeeded in their mission, at the cost of their lives. The antiaircraft gun behind the STZ-5 however, seems re-usable.

was surrounded and decided to push through after nightfall. Avoiding the road bridge, he launched his brigade across the damaged railway bridge, a little further north. His charge swept aside the *schützen* covering that exit. The colonel however had to leave behind several damaged tanks and more were lost during the crossing. On October 12, the 4th Brigade was reduced to three KV-1s, seven T-34s and 22 light tanks, as opposed to 60 a week earlier. But it had fulfilled its mission perfectly: the 1st Guards Rifle Corps had held a strong defensive line outside Mtsensk and on the Zusha. Whilst its losses remained low—87 killed since October 1—the 4th Panzer Division was unable to start a new offensive. The division was forced to pause operations for 15 days, which dealt a severe blow to the objectives set by Hitler. Tula, let alone Moscow, remained well out of reach. The new "Second Panzer Army" was immobilized at a crucial moment, due to logistics failures, the state of the roads and the Red Army's opposition. Stalin personally congratulated Katukov on the phone, but he was only allowed a few days' rest before being sent back to the front. A month later, Katukov was promoted major general and the 4th Brigade became the 1st Tank Brigade of the Guard.

The Colonel's Hour

On October 8, Hoepner's Fourth Panzer Army was posing a much greater threat to Moscow than the Second Panzer Army.

Indeed Guderian, despite his early success in Orel, was still far from Moscow. Conversely, Hoepner's front line was less than 200km away. Here the Mozhaysk Line proved its worth, and here too the Red Army possessed a particularly competent officer. On June 22, 1941, Colonel Semyon Bogdanov commanded the 30th Tank Division, soon almost annihilated by Guderian's panzers: it went from 243 tanks to 40 in the space of 24 hours. Receiving what was left of the 14th Mechanized Corps, he was then entrusted with the formation of new tank brigades. When, on October 5, the three fronts defending Moscow were encircled, he was appointed to command part of Mozhaysk's defensive sector, primarily in the 37th fortified zone whose keystone was situated around Borodino, 120km from Moscow. But apart from a few remnants of the Western Front, like the 50th Division near Gzhatsk, its only resources consisted of incomplete tank brigades sent from the RGVK (Reserve of the Supreme High Command). Bogdanov chose to use them to slow the German armored advance, while he waited for the promised reinforcements to arrive. The 18th Brigade (29 T-34s, 34 BTs and T-26s) reached Gzhatsk and the 17th (29 T-34s, 32 T-40s and a battery of 8 ZIS-30s) reached Maloyaroslavets to conduct the kind of mobile defense that had worked so well for Katukov and Lelyushenko. Three other brigades followed.

Bogdanov took the initiative and made some excellent decisions even before Zhukov's arrival. Due to planning mistakes and a surfeit of confidence, the German charge toward Moscow was led by just two motorized formations, because the panzer divisions of the Fourth Panzer Army were required to deal with the Vyazma pocket. In the south, the LVII Panzer Corps launched the 3rd Motorized Division towards Maloyaroslavets on the Warsaw–Moscow road, and east of Mozhaysk, the SS-Das Reich Division was the vanguard for the XL Panzer Corps. The 3rd Motorized Division took the bridgehead over the Ugra, won by the 10th Panzer Division, who was then regrouping near Vyazma.

On the 8th, a Russian motorized division reached the *frontoviki* holding the Warsaw–Moscow road. They were Captain Starchak's students from the Podolsk school, and the 17th

These obstacles on the edge of the capital are less elaborate than those in the town center.

To protect the Bolshoi Theater, what better way than a *trompe l'oeil* camouflage to trick the invader! The outline of the theater was painted on the facades of the square next to the theater to protect it from a direct hit, while the colonnade of the theater itself was disguised with settings from the opera *Prince Igor*.

Here is a tank from the 10th Company, taken from the Polish Army in 1939. The police's armored units first used captured machines, including Soviet ones from as early as the summer. Originally in charge of securing the rear, police units also took part in mass murder. For example, on September 1, a company from the Police Regiment Mitte killed 900 Jews in Minsk. (Bundesarchiv Bild 121-1207)

Brigade's motorized battalion. The commander of which, Commandant Nikolai Klypin, already a Hero of the Soviet Union, needed to gain enough time to destroy the various bridges on the road to Maloyaroslavets. The real attack started a day later, with the belated support of the Panzer 38(t)s from the 20th Panzer Division. The defense folded and towards the end of the day Klypin brought up two T-34 companies that clashed with Colonel Horst Wolff's 478th Infantry Regiment (258th Infantry Division) which had been sent to support—until now successfully—the 3rd Motorized Division. Unfortunately for him, the regiment only had 3.7cm Pak 35s and 36s, whose shells bounced off the Soviet armor. The T-34s scattered part of the regiment and Wolff was killed trying to rally his terrified men. The Russians managed to reach new positions west of Medyn. On the 10th, the 3rd Motorized Division exploited its infantry superiority to overwhelm the Russian positions, whilst still retaining pressure on the road. The Luftwaffe intervened *en masse*. It eliminated a few of the 17th Brigade's vehicles and allowed the Germans to get past the defenders. However, another counterattack from Klypin led to a disorderly retreat by the German infantry when they tried to cross the Medynka river at a ford. Once more the Russians fell back to the Mozhaysk Line, in front of Maloyaroslavets. The 312th Rifle Division, which had arrived in the meantime, came to reinforce the ranks of the Podolsk students, whilst two other rifle divisions gathered further back. The 17th Brigade lost two-thirds of its tanks, most of them simply damaged, and some just broken down, but abandoned due to an inability to repair. Nevertheless, the LVII Panzer Corps, forced to rebuild several destroyed bridges, was not able to launch its

One of the first T-34s brought back into service by the Germans.

offensive before the 12th, by which time it was attacking a fortified position. Klypin, just like Katukov, had played the role of "brake" well, slowing a numerically far superior opponent.

Similarly, in the north, on October 8, the SS-Das Reich marched on Mozhaysk. More powerful than the 3rd Motorized Division with three infantry regiments, its only armor consisted of a battery of six Sturmgeschütz and a few Panzerspähwagen. Gruppenführer Paul Hausser easily took Gzhatsk from the 50th Division the next day. He then sent his motorcyclist battalion, followed by the Der Führer Regiment towards Mozhaysk and Moscow. But Colonel Alexandr Druzhinina had positioned the tanks of his 18th Brigade in an ambush 10km east of Gzhatsk. Around 16:30, the armored cars and motorcyclists of the SS-Das Reich Division fell into the trap. With no antitank weapons other than their

Two *frontoviki*, looking determined on the road to Moscow. They are armed with an SVT-40 semi-automatic rifle and a DP-28 light machine gun. The urgency of the situation meant that the officer cadets and other units mobilized to stop the panzers after the encirclements had to make do with rough and ready equipment. (Ph. Rio Collection)

3.7cm guns, the SS fell back after suffering heavy losses. Hausser immediately requested support from the 10th Panzer Division. Still engaged in the Vyazma pocket, it could only spare its tank regiment, entrusted to its commander, Oberst von Hauenschild. Kampfgruppe Hauenschild left for Gzhatsk the next morning, comprising the 7th Panzer Regiment, 10th

Motorcycle Battalion, an artillery group, a pioneer company and a self-propelled 2cm Flak battery. At 13:00 the SS again went into combat, one panzer battalion supporting the Deutschland Regiment and another the Der Führer Regiment. Nevertheless Druzhinina, who had also received reinforcements—the 19th Brigade with 14 T-34s and KVs and 30 light tanks—held on. On the same day the 32nd Division arrived in Mozhaysk. Druzhinina continued to slow down the main force of the XL Panzer Corps, helped by the mud, which disrupted the deployment of the enemy's artillery. Hauenschild did manage to surround the 18th Brigade for a time; only seven tanks managed to get out. On the 13th, when the two brigades were finally allowed to leave the front, 75 percent of their tanks were missing. As for 7th Panzer Regiment, it left behind about 20 machines. However, Druzhinina had also fulfilled his mission. The 32nd Division, largely reinforced, had strongly positioned itself within the fortifications of the Mozhaysk Line, near Borodino, under command of the new 5th Army. Under the command of Lelyushenko, who had been recalled from Mtsensk where the situation was stabilizing, it only possessed a handful of units.

With Zhukov's arrival as head of the capital's defense, the Red Army slowly began to recover from the disaster of Vyazma-Bryansk. Whilst it was impossible to stop Army Group Center everywhere, the more crucial axes were now all defended, sometimes thanks to the initiative of quite junior officers, like Bogdanov, who became Lelyushenko's deputy. Zhukov now fielded 18 rifle divisions and 11 tank brigades against the front of Army Group Center. This "thin red line" remained fragile however, especially as other bad news came in, from Kalinin for instance. From mid-October, with the pockets being eliminated, Army Group Center was able to re-focus its resources towards the east and Moscow.

An Fw 189 "Uhu" (Eagle Owl) takes off from a snowy airfield. This excellent reconnaissance aircraft proved elusive prey for the Soviet fighters thanks to its maneuverability and robustness. (O. Walther Luben/ECPAD/Defense)

| Out of Breath

By mid-October, whilst the Soviet situation remained critical near Moscow, a defense was being put in place on the Mozhaysk Line. Everywhere Army Group Center was meeting resolute resistance. And though they often managed to prevail, the collapse of the Soviet regime did not appear imminent, with Ostheer forces being spread thinly over a vast area.

On the main axis, the pursuit started after the conclusion of *Typhoon*'s first phase was almost stillborn. Elsewhere, it slowed radically despite a weak opposition. The Second Panzer Army, probably the most hindered by the supply problems and the mud, had to wait until October 22 to attack Mtsensk and did not take Kursk before November 1. However, further north,

This Panzer IV Ausf. F negotiating a bog has an improvised but rather successful winter camouflage. Thanks to its short-barreled 7.5cm KwK 37 L/24, this tank excelled in infantry support and against enemy strongpoints, though it was not too efficient against T-34s. The 5cm KwK 38 L/42 of the Panzer III was not much better. (Bundesarchiv)

The frost made it easier to extract vehicles from the mud, but the situation often called for assistance from other vehicles, such as this Panzer II. (Jacobsen/ECPAD/Defense)

The advance towards Kalinin involved the 101st Flamethrower Panzer Battalion, equipped with standard Panzer IIs and IIIs but above all with Panzer II (F)s like this one. These small tanks had two flamethrowers mounted on each side of the bodywork, as seen here, even if the turret machine gun seems to be missing. The Panzer II (F) would prove formidable during the street fighting of October 14.

the Third Panzer Army and the Ninth Army continued their chase of the Western Front's remaining fragments, towards the northeast as planned. On the central axis Zhukov—still deeply worried—was actually only facing the Fourth Panzer Army and Fourth Army. Furthermore, Kluge progressed slowly and only one of his divisions was able to lend help to Hoepner against the Mozhaysk Line. Clearly opposed to the plans of Hitler and the OHK, the commander of the Fourth Army worried about a situation, which "undoubtedly hinders the continued advance of our weak attack groups." Poorly supplied, mired in the *rasputitsa*, facing an enemy who refused to give up, he believed the Germans should go onto the defensive. Consequently, Kluge deprived Hoepner of his support at a crucial time. Nevertheless, on the 14th, a new crisis began north of Moscow, when the Third Panzer Army pulled off a daring move.

Blitzkrieg on Kalinin

As the Vyazma pocket was reduced, three Soviet armies moved back toward the northeast. The 22nd Army tried to raise a coherent defense around Rzhev in order to prevent access

This close-up of a bunker in Ilinskoye shows a 45mm M1932 gun. Under the command of Lieutenant A. K. Deremjan, this bunker and its occupants yielded during the German assault, but inflicted losses on 5th Company, 27th Panzer Regiment.

This panzer, "512," has ended up in the ditch. Like most other Panzer 38(t)s here, it is an Ausf. E or F. Most of these wrecks, irreparable, were used as a source of spare parts. At least 11 soldiers of 27th Panzer Regiment lost their lives during this particular fight.

from the east and northeast. But the Germans exploited the confusion that prevailed amongst the Russian ranks, which was admittedly a mass of 15 under-strength divisions answering to five different armies. On the 10th, the 1st Panzer Division easily crushed the 247th Division, which had been considered solid as a third of it comprised Party members and/or NKVD. *Die Erste* (the First) captured 2,000 men and 40 guns, which was what was left of the division. The survivors joined the 250th Division and the 247th was officially disbanded. The XLI Panzer Corps exploited the breach and on the 11th, broke through northeast of Rzhev, while the Ninth Army infantry kept the pressure up west of the town. A large part of the 30th Army ended up surrounded. The discovery of an all-important Russian fuel depot helped compensate for the shortages suffered by XLI Panzer Corps. Its advance on Kalinin was made with *kampfgruppen*, more due to the lack of fuel than a tactical flexibility. The poor quality and the rarity of the roads, the insufficient supplies, and a few isolated *frontoviki* were the only problems met by the 1st Panzer Division. On the 13th, whilst Rzhev was being evacuated, Captain A. P. Sergeyev, commander of the 180th Fighter Regiment, took off in his MiG-3 to reach the base at Kalinin, in the south. He and his deputy landed on an airfield that appeared deserted, apart from some "strange vehicles." By the time they realized that these were German soldiers, Sergeyev was already trapped. His wingman managed to take off again, after shooting a *landser* who had climbed on his wing. Sergeyev was probably summarily executed—his body was found in December by Soviet soldiers. On the 14th, Kalinin, a city of more than 200,000 inhabitants, a little over 100km away from Moscow, fell. The 1st Panzer Division broke the Red Army's opposition with the panzers of the 101st Flamethrower Panzer Battalion and secured the city and its bridges over the Volga, less than 100km away from Moscow.

At Sergijevka the Russians rapidly brought the excellent 76.2mm and 85mm anti-aircraft guns into play against the panzers, with devastating effect. An 85mm K-52 like this one contributed to the carnage. In 1943, the Red Army put together antitank battalions equipped with this weapon to deal with the new German tanks, the Tiger and the Panther.

Kalinin's fall threatened to create a new breach in Zhukov's defenses and so he ordered his right wing to withdraw towards the capital. The news heightened Muscovites' fears, as Olga Sapozhninova recalls: "It felt like the Germans could turn up in the street at any time." The competent and aggressive General Nikolai Vatutin was given several units of the Northwestern Front to retake Kalinin. But the move to take the city, as sudden as it was audacious, fitted in with the increasingly absurd strategy of the Ostheer. Far from falling on Moscow, XL Panzer Corps had to leave for the northwest to assist an assault launched by Army Group North from the Novgorod district to destroy the Northwestern Front. This order no. 25 was confirmed by Hitler's own *aide de camp* who specified that: "what matters to the Führer is that before winter comes, as many enemy units as possible should be destroyed. To conquer more territories is not as important." Assigning such an objective to a meager army corps, poorly supplied and isolated at the end of the line, said a lot about the superiority complex that still reigned among the German command. This diversion towards Kalinin eased the pressure on Moscow's defenders. The advance of XLI Panzer Corps from Rzhev to Volokolamsk would have had disastrous effects. The only unit there was the inadequate and re-formed 16th Army, but under command of another rising star of the Red Army, Konstantin Rokossovsky. When, on the 16th, LVI Panzer Corps did approach, from Vyazma, reinforcements had already arrived.

In Profile:
Soviet Aircraft

Ilyushin Il-2, 502nd Ground-Attack
Regiment, Yukhnov sector, October 6, 1941.

Polikarpov R-5, 606th Light Bomber
Regiment, sector of Yukhnov, October 6, 1941.

Mikoyan-Gurevich MiG-3, Captain A.
P. Sergeyev, 180th Fighter Regiment,
Kalinin aerodrome, October 13, 1941.

When winter came, the Russian air force had the advantage of better bases, but also of equipment that was better adapted to the weather. This LaGG-3 has ski landing gear. The LaGG-3, whilst mediocre remained a robust machine. (G. Gorokhov Collection)

From Sergijevka's Pavement to Volokolamsk

West of Maloyaroslavets, General Kuntzen reorganized LVII Panzer Corps to seize the positions on the Mozhaysk Line. The 19th Panzer Division took over from the 3rd Motorized Division. The first attempts on the 12th, did not yield results, in fact quite the opposite, with the T-34s destroying three Panzer 38(t)s. The Germans exploited the Russian flanks' weakness, but the *rasputitsa* meant the attackers had to move along the axis of the road. After two days of slow progress, German firepower finally made the difference. The 3rd Battalion of the Podolsk School only had 180 cadets left, from 500 a week earlier. The 53rd

Rifle Division launched nighttime counterattacks but on the 15th, the front crumbled. The next day, Maloyaroslavets seemed within reach. First Lieutenant Wagner of the 19th Panzer Division, apparently said to his men: "Here, it's Maloyaroslavets, 19km away from where we are. It is there that our tanks must be tomorrow. And here is Podolsk, the division's objective for next week, 34km from Moscow [...] This is why we must crush these *blockhaus* from hell [in Sergijevka]. We must clear the road. The tanks cannot get through in the swamps and the infantry units that made progress in the south need supplies.[1]

The task was given to 5th Company, 27th Panzer Regiment, accompanied by riflemen, some transported in Sdkfz 251s, some simply on top of the tanks. This charge seemed suicidal, but the Germans thought that the Russian defenses were very weak and led attacks on the flanks in parallel to the main attack. At 12:00, the column of 15 panzers began its advance. Two were hit before reaching Ilinskoye, forcing most of the infantrymen to jump off their rides, but the others pushed all the way through to Sergijevka. There, they took heavy fire from artillery students of the Podolsk School. The clash ended in carnage and only one panzer came out intact. However, the infantry and a few panzers making their way around the flanks managed to neutralize the defenders. Another similar *kampfgruppe* followed suit towards the east and overcame Maloyaroslavets quite easily. The 43rd Army fell back to the Nara river, with amongst others, the remnants of the 17th Tank Brigade. Kuntzen had broken the Mozhaysk Line.

---

1   P. Carell.

Poorly armed and armored, inferior in many respects to the T-26 or other battle tanks, this Czech design was living its last moments as a combat tank in the panzer divisions. (Bundesarchiv 101I-268-0185-06A)

There were only a few Henschel Hs-123 available during Operation *Typhoon*, put to use by II (Schl)/LG2. It played an important role during the Kalinin offensive. It could shake free of the mud without too much problem, even when the landing gear fairings had to be removed, as in this photograph taken during the summer. (Bundesarchiv)

However the XLVI Panzer Corps had still not started its main assault against Volokolamsk. A rifle division, two tank brigades and two antitank regiments had time to arrive before it left its start line. General von Vietinghoff was slow to act, primarily due to logistics; and the worsening state of the roads was not helping. On October 18, the 2nd Panzer Division's infantry and artillery failed to cover more than 10km. The defenders took advantage of the panzers' limited mobility, as they were again forced to undertake frontal attacks. And when the German artillery started to run out of shells, or even guns, the Soviet pieces could be heard. Nevertheless, the 316th Division was decimated and the Germans captured several undamaged T-34s, their inexperienced crews abandoning them at the first sign of trouble. But the advance was reduced to another slow and painful progression; the Russians had received the welcome support of the 4th Brigade, though somewhat diminished after the Mtsensk battle. However the T-34s' wide tracks could better negotiate the mud than the Panzer IIIs and IVs. But eventually Volokolamsk fell, causing a new breach in the Mozhaysk Line, just 60km from Moscow.

The Black Order against the Red Star

By October 12, Hausser's SS-Das Reich was approaching Borodino. The battle that followed is often reduced to an almost symbolic fight between the SS and the "Siberians," both considered fanatic elite fighters. The reality is more nuanced. The 32nd Division had seen battle, but in 1938, against the Japanese. It was supported by several units, antitank regiments, Katyusha battalions, officer cadets, and new recruits, not forgetting the worn-out tank brigades. The defenses were even reinforced by the empty carcasses of old T-28s, dragged onto the battlefield to serve as blockhouses.

The first clash resulted in the loss of six panzers, which fell victim to the powerful 76.2mm F-22 guns. The day after, Hausser tried his luck without the support of the 10th Panzer Division, but with the Nebelwerfers and Stukas. Alone, the SS broke through the forward positions, exploiting the deficiencies of the fortified line, and the competence of their assault pioneers who opened up gaps in the barbed wire and destroyed more than one bunker with explosives and flamethrowers. Around the village of Artemki, the Der Führer Regiment attacked an officer cadet battalion, The Sons of Lenin, from the flank, and eliminated it. Hausser then brought forward his last regiment, the 11th SS-Infantry Regiment, and its battery of assault guns. Lelyushenko counterattacked with the 32nd Division's Reconnaissance Group, equipped with light tanks and armored cars, and supported by Colonel Timofei Orlenko's 20th Tank Brigade, just arrived, with 60 machines, including 29 T-34s. The latter started a panic within the SS, but Orlenko himself was killed by the very *frontoviki* he was trying to rally. Both sets of elite troops were decidedly showing some weaknesses. The SS-Das Reich Division had to return to its starting positions.

Hausser had to wait for the next day and the 10th Panzer Division, which at that time was fighting bitterly around the Borodino station. The panzers were nearing Lelyushenko's HQ, who was leading a counterattack in person—whilst charging, Molotov cocktail in hand, he was seriously wounded. The 76.2mm guns were proving to be formidable and blocked the panzers. Hausser himself was seriously wounded by shrapnel, and yielded command to

T-28s destroyed on a forest road. Unlike the T-34 and KV, these machines became rarer in the Red Army. Necessity ruled however, and these multi-turret tanks were still employed, the 32nd Rifle Division even using engineless T-28, as fortifications on the Borodino battlefield. (G. Gorokhoff Collection)

These gunners, manning a MG 34 on its heavy mount, are equipped in a typical manner for the first winter in USSR. The only camouflage visible is the white smock, possibly improvised. The hats are fur-lined, taken from the Russians. (Bundesarchiv 101I-268-0181-10)

Oberführer Wilhem Bittrich. On the Russian side, General Leonid Govorov took over from Lelyushenko. The German assault started again the next day. Snow had fallen overnight and now blanketed the region. Again, the Siberian riflemen pushed the 10th Panzer Division back, out of the Borodino station, then towards the end of the day, the 20th Brigade forced the Deutschland Regiment to retreat. But on the 17th, decimated, exhausted, the 32nd Division faltered and the panzers reached Borodino.

The next day, Kampfgruppe von Bülow entered Mozhaysk, abandoned by the 5th Army. The Russians were out of sight. As in 1812, the battle of Borodino had ended in a blood bath. The German divisions lost more than 2,000 men, the SS-Das Reich Division forced to dissolve the 11th SS-Infantry Regiment. The 10th Panzer Division lost 50 tanks—though a lot of them were only damaged they would not be repairable in the near future. On the Russian side, most of the tanks and more than 10,000 men were out of action, the 32nd Division having lost 50 percent of its numbers, more than 7,500 men, in the battle. The battle of Borodino in 1812 had also been a bloody struggle and it had opened the way to Moscow, but this was not the case in October 1941. The Mozhaysk Line had collapsed in several places and Army Group Center was getting closer to the capital, but it was also at the end of its tether.

| Afterword

In Moscow, the fall of Mozhaysk, more so than the fall of Kalinin, caused a new wave of panic. But Zhukov had won his bet. The Germans had used up their resources, wearing out their best units even further, without truly breaking through. The Fourth Panzer Army had received only 15–20 percent of its supplies, and the weather was continuing to worsen. The Russian opposition was not weakening either: the first counteroffensives around Kalinin began on the 17th and continued for several days. Moreover, the defenses built up in a hurry 50km away from the capital were now already occupied by some troops. Admittedly their quality varied, and the shortage of materiel was being felt more than ever, especially the tanks. Nevertheless, the 11 tank brigades sacrificed to slow the Germans down had played their part well. They had stalled the enemy sufficiently that there had been time to put a coherent front together. This was in large part thanks to young officers whose professionalism was inspirational to those serving with them. And if Army Group Center had never been closer to Moscow, the atmosphere in the Stavka and the Kremlin had shifted from the dark days of early October. On the 18th, as Mozhaysk fell, Stalin called Zhukov at his headquarters: "Are we sure we are holding Moscow?" Zhukov answered firmly in the affirmative. If the government was leaving, Stalin remained in the Kremlin and made it known.

At the end of this cold and damp October, the storm started by *Typhoon* seemed to be abating.

| Further Reading

Braithwaite, Rodric. *Moscow 1941: A City and its People at War*. London, UK: Profile Books, 2006.

Clark, Alan. *Barbarossa: The Russian German Conflict 1941–1945*. London, UK: Weidenfeld & Nicolson, 1995.

Cumins, Keith. *Cataclysm: The War on the Eastern Front 1941–45*. Solihull, UK: Helion, 2011.

Glantz, David M. *Operation Barbarossa: Hitler's Invasion of Russia 1941*. Tempus, 2001.

Harrison, Richard W. *The Battle of Moscow 1941–1942: The Red Army's Defensive Operations and Counter-Offensive along the Moscow Strategic Direction*. Solihull, UK: Helion, 2015.

Hoth, Hermann (trans. Linden Lyons). Panzer Operations: Germany's Panzer Group 3 during the Invasion of Russia, 1941. Philadelphia, PA: Casemate, 2015.

Nagorski, Andrew. *The Greatest Battle: The Battle for Moscow, 1941–42*. London, UK: Aurum Press, 2007.

Stahel, David. *The Battle for Moscow*. Cambridge, UK: Cambridge University Press, 2015.

Zetterling, Niklas and Anders Frankson. *The Drive on Moscow 1941: Operation Taifun and Germany's First Crisis of World War II*. Philadelpia, PA: Casemate, 2012.

Index